Counsel for Pastors' Wives

Counsel for Pastors' Wives

FOREWORD BY RUTH SENTER

DIANE LANGBERG

Ministry Resources Library

Zondervan Publishing House • Grand Rapids, MI

COUNSEL FOR PASTORS' WIVES
Copyright © 1988 by Diane Langberg

MINISTRY RESOURCES LIBRARY is an imprint of
Zondervan Publishing House
1415 Lake Drive, S.E.
Grand Rapids, Michigan 49506

Library of Congress Cataloging in Publication Data

Langberg, Diane.
    Counsel for pastors' wives / Diane Langberg.
       p.   cm.
    ISBN 0-310-37621-1
    1. Clergymen's wives—Pastoral counseling of. I. Title.
BV4395.L36 1988
248.8'92—dc19   87-30278
                                             CIP

Edited by Laura Dodge Weller
Designed by James E. Ruark

Printed in the United States of America

88 89 90 91 92 93 94 95 / EP / 10 9 8 7 6 5 4 3 2 1

To my husband, Ron,
whose love and encouragement
made this book and many other
ministry adventures possible

Contents

Foreword

I could almost feel the pain etched between the lines of the letter from a distraught pastor's wife in Indiana. I wanted to reach out and give her a hug, hop a plane and rush to her side, and fix her hurt for her. Instead, I sat behind my desk at the *Partnership* offices and wondered who might help. I went through my files and pulled out a similar letter from another pastor's wife. Stapled to it was a response from Diane Langberg.

From the first line of Diane's response I knew I had found someone who not only cared about hurting clergy but also knew how to communicate that care through her writing. Diane did not talk down to the hurting woman, but treated her with the greatest respect. She did not fill her response with "shoulds" and "oughts" or high-sounding lingo that only the professionals could understand. Instead, she was a comfortable friend pulling up a chair and coming alongside to encourage and give hope. Though she was thoroughly professional herself, I noted that Diane did not pass along simply her own opinions or the ideas of other professionals. She was not out to convince or impress with what she knew. Rather, she skillfully built upon biblical principles, weaving eternal truths into sound professional advice and practical application.

I knew I could not personally help the hurting

pastor's wife from Indiana whose letter I held in my hand. But I had found someone who could. I folded the letter and sent it to Diane, confident that I had been of special service to a pastor's wife who needed an understanding friend and counselor.

Today, several years removed from that letter, I am more convinced than ever that Diane Langberg truly loves clergy couples and understands their unique position. She has offered hope and help to many through the pages of *Partnership*. May I be the first to introduce her to you through the pages of this book. She is my friend, and by the time you have finished reading *Counsel for Pastors' Wives,* she will be your friend too.

Ruth Senter
October 1987

Acknowledgments

This book began about ten years ago when the first distraught pastor and his wife walked into my office for counseling. Many such couples have passed through my life since then in counseling sessions, in conferences, and in letters to the *Partnership* "Counselor." It has been a privilege to counsel these people.

I am grateful to Ruth Senter and the staff of *Partnership*, who provided me with the opportunity to minister to many pastors' wives through the "Counselor" column.

I appreciate the courage of the women who have asked for guidance. Their letters have been rewritten to protect their identities, but the problems presented and questions asked are theirs.

Many thanks to Georgia Hardiman and Holly Bush for their typing skills.

I would like to extend special thanks to my friend and editor Michael Smith, whose patience and excellent suggestions enabled me to keep the vision of a finished product ever before me.

Dear Diane,

I have a concern about my pastor husband that I have not seen mentioned in any of the literature for those in the ministry. Perhaps it is an uncommon problem, but I do not think so. Several times a week my husband drinks at home or at a local bar. He sometimes stays at the bar until very late. I am terrified that one of the members of our church might see him. His credibility as a pastor could be questioned, his drinking could have an adverse effect on a new Christian, and drinking is frowned upon in our denomination. His father, also a pastor, would be very distressed if he knew. My husband calls this his recreation, but I see it as dangerous. If he were in any other profession, perhaps the consequences might not be so great, but in the ministry the discovery of his drinking could affect our lives drastically. He listens to nothing I say. What should I do?

Sincerely,
Beth

(Note that the letter appearing on this page should be on page 94, and the letter on page 94 should be on this page.)

CHAPTER 1
Can My Husband and I Survive the Pastorate?

Problems in the ministry seem almost fashionable today. The trials of clergy and their families are becoming increasingly a focus of concern among seminary and denominational administrators. I have counseled many aspiring pastoral couples who find the negatives they are hearing about frightening and even overwhelming. When one hears about burnout, broken marriages, mixed-up kids, and divided churches, one certainly can get the feeling that clergy couples risk losing more than they gain by their service to the church.

Whenever I conduct a seminar on ministry and its areas of difficulty, I am careful to acknowledge that I am proceeding from the "down side." Much of what I say focuses on *problems* simply because those who visit my office come because of difficulties and questions they cannot resolve. Even in the most solid of pastoral marriages there may be recurring problems or patterns commonly shared by others in ministry. All clergy marriages must deal with tension between ministry and family. Ministry couples must also learn to live with a job that is *never* done; no matter what is accomplished, new needs arise and must be met. They struggle with living up to others' expectations, with having the church determine their income, and with having their house belong to others and used as an extension of the church. These issues all contribute to the strain on pastoral marriages and result in frightening divorce statistics. More men are leaving the ministry due to discouragement and more ministry couples are divorcing than ever before.

Over my past ten years of counseling ministry couples, the majority of problems presented to me have usually fallen into one of two large categories: marriage/family difficulties or burnout. Struggles in those areas must be expected due to the type of work involved in the ministry and because of its intensity. These struggles do not need to be debilitating, however, nor must they inevitably result in the failure of either marriage or ministry. Whether or not problems get out of hand is in large measure dictated by the attitudes and expectations with which one approaches ministry.

I gladly will share with you my thoughts on both these areas. I do this to encourage you in your ministry rather than to frighten you with its negative possibilities. I pray that the joy of serving God in his church may be your first and most precious discovery in a new pastorate.

Let's look at marriage/family difficulties first. Many times couples feel as if marriage is in conflict with ministry. The attitude seems to be: "If I really give to my marriage what all these books and counselors say I should, my ministry will suffer. Marriage is important, but my ministry is for God, and he deserves 100 percent." This type of thinking translates into the resolve that "I will respond to anyone who calls at any time. If I have promised my wife that I will stay home, she will just have to understand that God's work comes first."

Perhaps the bluntness of the above statement makes it seem like something that you would never say. However, this type of thinking can creep in subtly. The reason for this error is a misunderstanding of how marriage and ministry fit together. Many couples believe and *live* as if marriage and ministry do not fit together. They view these two areas as being in irresolvable conflict and feel that one must be subordinate. Frequently, this translates into a severe neglect of the family, because "serving the Lord" is more important. Those having this attitude define service to God as "those spiritual things that take place outside the home."

Other couples believe that marriage and ministry ought somehow to fit together, so they run back and forth between the two. The fit is never comfortable or easy, but they enjoy some success from their juggling efforts.

The first approach, a neglect of the home, is clear disobedience to God's standards for those who oversee his church. Paul tells us that "[an overseer] must manage his own family well" (1 Tim. 3:4). Obviously, a pastor cannot manage his home if he is never present. The second approach will not work when both areas make major demands at the same time. Those who try to take on both equally are prime candidates for burnout.

There is a better way. I have seen it work for people who made a commitment to it from the beginning, as well as for those who first chose one of the above approaches and then struggled hard to change horses in midstream. This third option regarding marriage and ministry is that we view our marriage as *part* of our ministry. Just as we view our Bible studies, our singing in the choir, our teaching, or our counseling as a part of our ministry, so we must see our marriage as a viable part of our service to God.

One of the most important assets in an effective ministry is a healthy and strong marriage. Many people in ministry are failing God because of problems in their homes that have been generated by their neglect.

One of the traps that many ministry couples have fallen into is that of separating spiritual things from earthly or mundane things. God makes no such distinction in our lives. We are to honor him and give glory to him in *everything* we do. Surely God would not have us neglect our families for the sake of his church. Rather, we need to nurture our relationships at home so they, by example, can strengthen the body.

An example of this is found in a young pastor who believed that the things he deemed "spiritual" must be treated as being more important than those he felt were of this world. Early in his ministry he worked six long days in the church. On his "day off" he left his wife and three small children at home and spent twelve hours in the streets passing out Bibles. This pattern was repeated for ten years, and his marriage and family suffered greatly. He said to me, "How I wish I had understood that loving my wife and nurturing my children were also ministries!" How we must grieve God when we neglect the very relationship that is to illustrate Christ's relationship to his bride. What is a greater affront is that we do it "in his name."

Several years ago I was counseling a ministry couple whose marriage was on the verge of breaking up. This pastor's neglect of his family was staggering. When I suggested to him that his pattern of behavior was not of God, he replied: "You do not understand. Whatever crosses my path is from God and requires my complete attention. I cannot say no. He will care for my family." This minister had defined ministry as absence from the home. How sad it is that he never saw that his family had also crossed his path and that his ministry to them was as important as any speaking engagement!

Everything we do is to glorify God, and all that we strive for is to be in service to him. This is as true of listening to and encouraging our spouse as it is of being at the bedside of a dying parishioner. God makes no distinctions: "And *whatever* you do, whether in word or deed, do it *all* in the name of the Lord Jesus" (Col. 3:17, italics mine).

The idea that every area of our lives is to be considered service to God is powerfully emphasized by Peter's exhortation to elders. He says that overseers are to shepherd others while also serving as examples to their flocks. Paul reiterates this idea many times when he says, "Copy me"; "Be imitators of me." We are to be godly examples to those we serve. This certainly includes all areas of home and family life as well as all aspects of our church ministry. A perfect ministry and a perfect marriage are not necessary in order to glorify God. However, obedient hearts that strive to please God in every area of life are necessary if our example is to bring honor to the name of Christ.

Not surprisingly, the second problem area, burnout, is often related to difficulties in marriage. Rarely have I met a man who had given up his ministry in desperation who had a healthy, successful marriage. A good marital relationship provides a haven for couples in the midst of the pressures and struggles of ministry. A marriage that has been honored and lovingly nurtured provides wonderful support during difficult times.

In addition to a sound marriage, there are certain attitudes and mind-sets that are crucial to weathering storms. The ministry is fertile ground for burnout partly because of its intensity, partly because it is a field where one serves unpredictable and often ungrateful people.

There are two aspects to the kind of attitude that will help us not only to avoid burnout, but also to serve with joy.

The first is found in 1 Kings 10:9. The queen of Sheba came to see for herself whether Solomon was all he was cracked up to be. After spending time with Solomon, she responded by acknowledging the source of Solomon's authority: "Praise be to the LORD your God, who has delighted in you and placed you on the throne of Israel. Because of the LORD's eternal love for Israel, he has made you king, to maintain justice and righteousness." God put Solomon on the throne to be king for *him*, to fulfill *his* purposes in others' lives.

Burnout often occurs when we forget that we live under authority—that we are subject to God and are accountable to him. Knowledge of this principle gives confidence. Our confidence should not rest solely in abilities, successes, intelligence, or schooling. Our confidence is to be rooted in God who rules and who has chosen us, redeemed us, forgiven us, and gifted us, and then placed us according to *his* purposes.

I counseled a pastor who was deeply depressed and convinced that his ministry of forty years was worthless. As a young man he had started a new work that had grown dramatically, and many had come to Christ through his ministry. In later years its management had been given over to others who had not

18

handled things responsibly, and the work died. This pastor's confidence had come to rest in the visible successes of his work. When the work died, he died emotionally as well, convinced that his value to God's kingdom was destroyed.

On the other hand, I know a loving and powerfully effective pastor who is not seminary trained. With some help he has lost the defensiveness he carried for so many years and has truly come to understand that confidence lies not in academic degrees but in God who has gifted him and called him.

Pressure is inevitable in the ministry. There are difficulties and disappointments. There are the overwhelming needs of others, questions for which we have no answers. And there are failures as well—both in our families and among our church leaders. If we do not find the confidence that comes from knowing that it is *God* who has placed us where we are, we will be crushed by the demands and responsibilities of leadership. We will buckle under the pressure. If, however, we recognize that our confidence lies in the fact that God has placed us where he has, for the purpose of conforming us to his Son, then we can respond by walking in obedience to him on all fronts. The result is that we can serve as examples to the flock.

The second aspect of an attitude that will help prevent burnout is the knowledge that, not only has *God* placed us, but it is *God* whom we serve. Keeping this key point in mind will prevent us from becoming exasperated with those to whom we minister.

Recently a pastor's wife who was struggling with bitterness and frustration with the ministry came to see me. She had been active in the church, leading groups and counseling women. Then a conflict arose in the church, and several women whom she had counseled lovingly and over a long time period spoke against her and her husband. Her response was to isolate herself from all aspects of the church. She had not yet learned the principle Paul gives us in Ephesians 5:1—2: "Be imitators of God, therefore, as dearly loved children, and live a life of love, just as Christ loved us and gave himself up for us as a fragrant offering and sacrifice to God."

One of the most difficult things about ministering to others is dealing with the response you will get (or fail to get) from them. You will stand by a parishioner when everyone else is against him or her, and at the budget meeting this very person will stand up and say, "The pastor gets too much money." You will counsel many hours with someone, and there will be no change. Disapproval, criticism, and rejection are very difficult in any circumstance, but when they follow loving, careful service, the pain can be overwhelming.

The key to weathering this frustration and pain has been given to us by the apostle Paul. The mainspring of Paul's ministry was not love for the church (though certainly that was present); it was love for Jesus Christ. Dr. Oswald Chambers, in *My Utmost for His Highest,* expounds on this principle:

> If we are devoted to the cause of humanity, we shall soon be crushed and brokenhearted, for we shall often meet with more ingratitude from men than we would from a dog; but if our motive is love to God, no ingratitude can hinder us from service to our fellowman.

As we lay down our lives for others in obedience to Christ we can serve unstintingly and joyfully, and we can be assured that his response to our obedience will be one of pleasure and love.

It is my prayer that these insights will further equip you and your husband to serve God in your home and in his church with great joy. Paul says, "If anyone sets his heart on being an overseer, he desires a noble task" (1 Tim. 3:1). Go forward expectantly into that work remembering that "if . . . God so commands, you will be able to stand the strain" (Exod. 18:23).

Dear Diane,

I am a young pastor's wife and am struggling for some balance in the area of intimacy within the body. Scripture tells us to share our burdens and confess our sins to each other. I am confused as to how that applies to me. Sometimes I feel people are truly interested in praying for me and supporting me. At other times I sense an unconstructive curiosity about "the pastor's wife."

How much should I talk about the sins I fight against? How do I keep from hurting those who are weaker? Many other pastors' wives with whom I have spoken say that I should share nothing unless it is with God or with my husband. Is this so? I would appreciate some guidelines for this area.

Sincerely,
Karen

CHAPTER 2

Should I Share My Struggles With Others in the Congregation?

The question you have raised is frequently asked by pastors' wives. It is difficult to find a balance between honesty and silence regarding our own struggles— the big challenges we face and the sinful nature at work in us. We do not want what we share to cause another to stumble.

In order to answer your question effectively, we must first look at how Scripture deals with the sins of God's leaders. It is clear that God does not expect the sins of those who lead his people to be hidden. Scripture tells us of men and women who loved and served God yet failed in some way.

The apostle Paul tells us in 1 Corinthians 10 why the history of God's people has been written: "These things happened to them as examples, and were written down as warnings for us. . . . No temptation has seized you except what is common to man . . ." (vv. 11, 13). These verses lay a foundation that can help us determine when and for what purpose we should be transparent before others regarding our own struggles. The following three guidelines can aid us in deciding whether openness is appropriate.

First, ask whether your openness will help others to see that God never allows us to be tempted beyond what we are able to bear. Often we become discouraged or seek to excuse our own behavior by saying that our struggle is unique. We rationalize that no one else faces such difficulties or that our burden is beyond our ability to cope. God says that our temptations *are* common to man and that we *are* able to endure them, for he has provided a way of escape. We need to be reminded of this frequently—not so much by hearing these facts stated but rather by seeing and hearing that other Christians are also struggling. If done properly, the shared experience of difficulty will encourage rather than discourage weaker Christians.

Often a leader's openness is more influential than anyone else's. People tend to assume that those in leadership are stronger or more spiritual. This leads to the conclusion that any good example a leader might provide is irrelevant to others' lives. Leaders sometimes contribute to this false assumption by their belief that they must present only the victorious side of the Christian walk.

A woman who taught a large Bible class was perceived by many to never experience discouragement or defeat. It was known to many that her husband was up for a promotion. He did not get it, and after much prayer, she opened the doors to her own battle with disappointment and anger. She did this in an honest but careful way that served to encourage many others in their own difficulties.

Scripture presents both the negative and positive sides of the Christian walk, and so must we—*but* we need to do it as purposefully as God does. The purpose of the honesty of Scripture regarding the failures of God's people is not simply to make us feel better or to satisfy our curiosity. Rather, its purpose is to help us grow in grace. There is weakness in all of us that, if shared indiscriminately, would not accomplish God's purpose. We must discuss only those things that will further the unity of the body and the equipping of the saints.

The second guideline for deciding whether to be open about our struggles is based on Paul's teaching in Ephesians 4:29: "Do not let any unwholesome talk come out of your mouths, but only what is helpful for building others up according to their needs, that it may benefit those who listen." We need to examine this verse from two points of view—our own and our listener's. We share things for one of two reasons: because our help is needed by a fellow believer or because we need another to come alongside and support or advise us. Both our giving of help by sharing our struggles and our seeking of help from the body need to be governed by the same guidelines. We are to say nothing that would serve as a detriment to someone's spiritual health. We are to speak only about that which will uplift, improve, or teach those who hear it. We must continually ask ourselves, "Does my sharing of this sin or struggle act as a catalyst for growth?" God has gifted his children to minister to one another, and we must be ready - to give and receive help, handling all situations in a manner that will encourage the body as it "grows and builds itself up in love" (Eph. 4:16).

The way is often cloudy here, for we are not always aware of what motivates us to share with others. We are tempted to talk about a struggle so that we will be accepted or better liked. Sometimes we hope

simply to be understood or not perceived as so intimi-
dating. At other times we decide to speak just for the
purpose of making someone feel better. These reasons
alone are not sufficient motives for sharing our struggles with sin. The only scriptural reason for such
openness is that the hearing of it will result in growth
in grace for the listener. This may mean that we will be
silent about some struggles simply because we are in a
position of leadership.

In the past, the ideal has been for leaders to share
nothing of their difficulties. Today there seems to be
more of a tendency in the other direction. Many
leaders seem inclined to share just to prove that they
are as bad as the rest of us! We must be careful here.
The consequences of a leader's action and revelations
can be great. There will be things that could have been
more readily shared by someone not in a leadership
position. This can prove difficult and will sometimes
make the way lonely. However, our personal needs
must not be the determining factor in what and how
much we share.

In all situations we must decide, with the help of
the Holy Spirit, whether our openness will serve as an
encouragement to the hearers as well as to ourselves.
We must be willing for God to use specifics concerning
our past or present struggles to edify and teach fellow
believers, but we must share only within the bound-
aries he has given. Some things can be shared but only
with a few who can be trusted to be silent and pray. I
know of one church where two of the elders' wives see
their specific ministry as listening ears and prayer
partners for the pastor's wife. What a blessing!

The third and final principle is found in the
question "Will what I say glorify God?" Listen to Paul
again: "We have this treasure in jars of clay to show
that this all-surpassing power is from *God* and not

from us. . . . All this is for your benefit, so that the grace that is reaching more and more people may cause thanksgiving to overflow *to the glory of God*" (2 Cor. 4:7, 15, italics mine). The overriding directive for Christians is that *everything* we say and do must glorify God. We are to bear one another's burdens to the glory of God, and we are to speak to the glory of God. Our openness or lack of it is to have as a direct consequence the fact that it glorifies God.

Paul says earlier in 2 Corinthians 4, "We do not preach ourselves, but Jesus Christ as Lord . . ." (v. 5). Guided by the philosophy that transparency and vulnerability are always good, many Christians preach themselves and their experience, good and bad. Transparency is good only if it is for the purpose of lifting up Christ as Lord. I have seen churches unified and encouraged in their growth as a pastor has shared his pain and struggle over something in his life.

One pastor who had never shared personal conflicts with anyone decided to tell his congregation of the fear and grief he experienced when he learned that his wife had cancer. He allowed them to see his turmoil as well as his continuing belief that all he had taught them about God was still true, regardless of his circumstances. The impact was powerful.

I have also seen churches hurt and people confused when some Christian's experience with sin was exposed. A Christian woman indiscriminately shared her husband's past struggles with adulterous relationships. As a result, he had to step down from his position as an elder. He had confessed the sin, and it was many years behind him. Her sharing, which she said she did to help others, caused many to stumble and incapacitated her husband as an elder.

Obviously, there is no easy answer, and each situation must be decided separately. We do not want others to see us as anything other than earthen vessels, but the purpose for making that known is that they may see that "the surpassing greatness of the power" is of God and not from ourselves. We do not want to hide our pain and difficulties so that we miss God's blessing on us through his body, but we always want such openness to result in a preservation of the unity of that body. We do not want to be ruled by what others will think, yet we must care about their response to us, for we do not want to cause them to stumble. It is a difficult balance indeed, and it requires great wisdom. I am grateful that God has foreseen the difficulty and endowed us with his Spirit who will guide us into all truth.

Dear Diane,

I have always believed that expressing feelings honestly is an important asset to any relationship. My parents taught and demonstrated an openness about emotions. However, now I find myself in a confusing situation. I am married to a minister who is the son of a minister, and his background is very different from mine. He was taught that emotions are private and are not to be displayed. Even beyond that, his parents believe that expressing feelings is somehow destructive to God's work. They taught, and my husband believes, that any feeling that could possibly be viewed as negative should never be shared. He strongly believes that Christian leaders should keep their feelings to themselves. His world is one of theology, books, and Greek.

I strongly feel a need to express my feelings with my husband as well as with one or two carefully chosen friends. Should I, for the ministry's sake, pretend I don't have feelings or a need to share them? How can I let my husband know of my need to share my feelings when he won't even acknowledge having any? Any suggestions or new perspectives would be appreciated.

Sincerely,
Sue

CHAPTER 3

Can I Be Honest
About My Feelings?

Several years ago I counseled an adolescent boy who
had gotten into some very serious trouble. He was the
son of a minister, and he had some very angry feelings
toward his father that were rooted in his belief that his
father expected perfection from him. This belief stem-
med from his father's never allowing him to express
negative feelings. The boy said, "If I'm angry, sad,
frustrated, or discouraged, I dare not say. My father is
always disappointed when I have those feelings. He
never seems to have them. I guess I'll never be the man
he is."

Fortunately, the story had a happy ending, as
father and son learned to express themselves to one
another more openly and constructively. I mention it
because I think this boy's difficulty with his father and
yours with your husband are very similar.

Many Christians are pulled to one extreme or the
other regarding this issue of feelings. Some say that

all negative feelings indicate a lack of spirituality and should not be shared. Others say that whatever you feel should be expressed, and they offer no guidelines for determining what is helpful and what is not.

The subject of emotions and what to do with them is a frequently discussed topic that has polarized many Christians. In searching for a proper perspective, it is important not to go to one extreme or the other—either denying emotion or giving it free rein. Our answers to questions in this area must be rooted in Scripture rather than in our culture or simply in our own experience.

Though Scripture does not tell us why we were created with the capacity to feel, it does make clear that our emotionality is rooted in the nature and character of God. He is described as having emotions such as anger (Deut. 29:20), jealousy (Ps. 78:58), and delight (Isa. 62:4); and we are made in his likeness. However, who we are has been distorted by the Fall, so we cannot assume that our emotions are always proper nor that they come from a pure heart. Because of the Fall, emotions can be sinful and destructive to others. But this does not mean that all emotions are now wrong or that all emotions should be repressed.

Scripture gives us many examples of God's people and the emotions they experienced. Consider David, a man of intense emotions. His psalms are authentic expressions of faith and feeling, both to God and to the people of God. David expresses feelings of anguish (55:4—5), weariness (69:3), and anxiety (94:19). On the other hand, he danced so exuberantly as an expression of his joy that his wife complained of his lack of dignity. Since we believe that all Scripture is inspired and profitable for training us in righteousness, we must assume this to be so regarding David's emotional expressions, not all of which are praiseworthy.

In the Gospels we see strong emotion in our Lord, who was made in the likeness of men. Though exactly what Christ felt is not stated, his action of overturning tables and driving out the money changers from the temple was not a flat, emotionless deed. His sadness at the death of his friend Lazarus was evident in his tears. His pain at Israel's rejection of him is strongly felt in his words, "O Jerusalem, Jerusalem . . ." (Matt. 23:37). He shared his distress and grief with Peter, James, and John in Gethsemane. It is partly our knowledge of these experiences that enables us to confidently approach a High Priest who can sympathize with our weaknesses (Heb. 4:15—16).

Paul and Peter and other Scripture writers show us the emotional struggles of those who loved and served God. Paul says in 2 Corinthians 1:8: "We do not want you to be uninformed . . . about the hardships we suffered. . . . We were under great pressure far beyond our ability to endure, so that we despaired even of life." In chapter 7 he says, "We were harassed at every turn—conflicts on the outside, fears within. But God, who comforts the downcast, comforted us by the coming of Titus . . ." (vv. 5—6). Here Paul says that he wants others to know what he felt and how overwhelming it was. He also wants them to know that God met his need at that time by sending comfort in the person of Titus. Paul reveals several negative emotions—conflicts, fears, and depression—and goes on to give glory to God for his provision in a fellow human.

These verses suggest some guidelines you might follow in handling your emotions. First of all, Paul shared his feelings with those he served. So it seems that there is a proper time and place to express negative feelings. Paul evidently determined this to be both proper and edifying. We must ask ourselves then: "What makes this expression good? Can we assume that all sharing of feelings, negative and positive, is good?"

In both of the above passages the revealing of Paul's emotions is followed by his giving glory to God. This is an important key. The ultimate concern for Christians is to glorify God, not merely to ventilate feelings or to share emotions. Emotional expression can be positive and even necessary, but it must be subservient to glorifying God. Paul goes on in 2 Corinthians 1 to honor God who delivered him and on whom he has set his hope. In chapter 7 Paul describes God as our great Comforter. In between, we find statements like 4:7: "But we have this treasure in jars of clay to show that this all-surpassing power is from God and not from us."

We can conclude from this verse that a sharing of our feelings can be good so long as it is governed by whether or not God will be glorified. This certainly does not mean that we should say everything we think and feel but rather that we should speak without a critical spirit, bitterness, or revenge ruling us. We are, as James has said, to be "quick to listen, slow to speak." (1:19). However, we are free within the limits of Scripture to share our feelings, and God has enabled others of his servants to glorify him in their precious ability to comfort us.

Several years ago I counseled a young woman who felt everything very intensely. Her husband, she claimed, was cold and unresponsive to her emotions. What evolved, however, was a picture of a woman who compulsively expressed every thought and feeling many times over until her husband felt forced to pretend coldness and disinterest. Her barrage of emotion was uncontrolled and caused much distance between them.

Another woman presented a similar problem: she

had a husband who was uninterested in her feelings. However, upon further questioning over several weeks, I found that when she said, "I need to share my feelings," that was accurately translated as "I need to tell my husband everything he did wrong."

Just because we feel something, no matter how strongly, it does not necessarily follow that it needs to be expressed. Some experts encourage us to express whatever we feel. God's Word acknowledges that we have feelings but calls on us to see that they are governed. Scripture teaches that feelings can be expressed, but we must do so according to the guidelines given to us.

If our emotions are either denied or given free rein, we will not glorify God. Many of us live on one side of the fence by wallowing in our emotions. We exercise no discipline over them and allow them to run our lives. We talk about them too much, resign ourselves to their influence, and make no attempt to glorify God through them.

On the other hand, many Christians believe it is spiritual not to have or not to show negative feelings. They are considered a weakness. It is as though we must hide our humanity in order to honor God. This presents a false picture of God at work in our lives and may lead others to conclude that we are simply made of stronger stuff, rather than that God has met our needs, for they see none. It also hinders those whom God has gifted in comforting others from exercising that gift in our lives. Our treasure is in earthen vessels, and that fact is not to be hidden, that the life of Jesus might be manifested in our body, bringing glory to God.

C. S. Lewis said that "Satan sends sin into the world in pairs of opposites." In this area, as in so many others, we see the need for the balance that is in Christ.

Your letter gives no indication to me that you are handling your emotions or struggles unwisely. You show caution and concern for when and how you express your feelings. I believe that you should continue sharing with your husband and carefully chosen friends. When possible, the level of intensity and certainly the repetition should be governed as you talk with your husband. Do not force the issue with him, for you cannot make him share with you. Try to make your talks such that he will not feel judged for not sharing in return. This will be particularly difficult when you sense his judgment for having shared your feelings. Your openness with him, if done carefully, may enable him to be more comfortable with feelings as well as with the possibility of sharing his own. Keep in mind that when a person grows up in a home where feelings are not easily expressed, to do so feels awkward and even wrong.

In your husband's case, this is emphasized by his belief that expressing negative feelings is not only uncomfortable, but sinful as well. Hence he perceives you as encouraging him in wrongdoing.

Your task is not to convince your husband of the rightness of your position but rather to accept him where he is. Continual disagreement with him over the handling of emotions will probably further entrench him in his position. You might more effectively share your feelings with your husband in the context of a prayer time together.

This can be done in two ways. First, when it is appropriate, pray openly about your disagreement in this area. Ask God to guide you both so you can better learn to meet each other's needs, but above all that you will do so in a way that glorifies Him. Second, you might let your husband know when something is troubling you. Seek his advice and his prayer support.

You may also find that he will discuss his own struggles more readily in the context of prayer. Let your husband know that you believe that God has given you to him as his helper or as one who can help to meet his needs. Make it clear that your desire is to bring glory to God by effectively ministering to your husband. Perhaps God will use your loving, uncritical example to enable your husband to share more of himself with you.

Dear Diane,

My husband and I have been in the ministry for many years. We are both in our fifties and have been in good health all our lives. During a recent exam, however, my husband's doctor found symptoms of what appears to be a mild form of a neurological disease. He advised us to see a neurologist, but my husband has chosen not to do so.

We have no savings and only a skeleton insurance policy. We are fearful that confirmation of the diagnosis will increase our premiums. We also fear that if our supporting churches found out, our financial support would be cut. We see no future in the ministry if it is discovered that my husband might be ill.

I am feeling great guilt over our silence. Out of loyalty to my husband I feel I must honor his wishes to keep quiet. He feels fine physically, and our work is going well. Should I cover for my husband? What about the conflict I feel between my loyalty to him and my sense of responsibility to the church? When should a wife act on her own convictions when they run counter to her husband's wishes?

Sincerely,
Liz

CHAPTER 4
Where Does My Loyalty Lie?

In reading of your dilemma I sense much anxiety and fearfulness. I am sure that you are concerned about what might be happening to your husband, what the future may hold for you, as well as whether or not you are wrong in your loyalty to your spouse. Your active and fulfilling ministry of many years seems threatened.

To be helpful, we must directly tackle the issue of loyalty to spouse versus personal convictions. However, in order to do that most effectively, we must first look at three aspects of your letter that concern me.

First, it appears that your anxiety has gained control over you. This happens from time to time to all of us, and we end up feeling anxious about things far removed from what the facts are. What you *know* is that the result of an exam indicated that *perhaps* your husband has a neurological disease. The diagnosis has not been confirmed by a specialist. However, your anxiety has caused you to worry about increased insurance rates and churches cutting your support and questioning the effectiveness of your service to them. You are trying to cope emotionally with all of these burdens, when, in fact, they are not yet a reality in your life.

How difficult it is for us not to be anxious for tomorrow. When Christ admonished us about this in Matthew 6, I am sure he did so for many reasons, one being that God does not give grace for what is not a reality in our lives. His grace is in proportion to our need for today. Today you have a frightening "if" in your life—but you do not have a certainty, nor are you being rejected by your churches and losing their financial support. What a great discipline it is to "destroy speculations . . . and take every thought captive to the obedience of Christ" (2 Cor. 10:5 NASB).

When this anxiety is conquered so that it no longer rules you, you must move on to the second area of concern—communication with your husband. Not knowing whether your husband has a debilitating disease is causing some real and justified anxiety. This may be affecting your marriage in a variety of ways. How do you feel about your husband's failure to follow the doctor's advice? Are you relieved because you do not want to know if the diagnosis is correct? Are you angry because you feel that your husband has stuck his head in the sand at a time when you need certainty? Have you let him know how you feel and what you believe is a wise course of action?

During this difficult time it is important that you carefully think through how you feel, how you would like to proceed, and what your expectations for your husband are. These concerns must be communicated to him in a loving, uncritical way, keeping in mind that he, too, is afraid. As you struggle through this together, with tears and much holding and encouraging of each other, ask God to make you of one heart and mind regarding how to proceed. Ask him to quiet the unnecessary fears, and ask for wisdom to discern his course of action. You may discover that it is a mistaken diagnosis. Or you may find that it is correct and that God will pour out untold blessings on your ministry through this affliction. If it should prove to be a correct diagnosis, God has ordained it. It may progress so slowly that it will not affect your ministry in any way for years and years. Or, if its course begins to alter your ministry, is it not conceivable that God will use it to teach and bless many whose lives you might not otherwise have touched?

Finally, I am concerned in regard to your attitude toward the churches that you serve. You seem to expect that should some disaster fall upon you and your husband, they will retreat, withdraw all financial support, and question the continued effectiveness of your ministry. Certainly human nature is capable of all of the above. However, isn't it quite possible that at least some people would consider you part of the body and look for ways to minister to you? Would your mission organization and these specific churches turn you out without support, emotional or financial, in a time of crisis? It is a sad commentary on the body of Christ if this is so. Perhaps you and your husband need to learn to share more of your needs with your churches and allow them the privilege of learning to serve you.

You and your husband likely will have to do a lot of communicating, crying, and praying before you can justifiably deal with the question of conflicting loyalties. If, after wrestling through your personal responses to the situation and discussing these areas at great length with your husband, you still find that you are in conflict, *then* your struggle in this realm becomes your priority.

Scripture emphasizes unity in marriage when it talks about the idea of one-fleshness. Husband and wife are to walk together in the same direction. They are not to pull in separate ways, with one undermining the other. The life that a husband and wife share and the dance that they do together are to demonstrate clearly the unity of Christ and his church. That leaves little room for anything divisive, such as sarcastic barbs or parting ways.

On the other hand, Scripture is very clear that our first loyalty is, without question, to God himself. Our relationship to him and our obedience to his Word are to be above any other priority in our lives. When anyone or anything would lead us to disobey him, we must obey God and not man—even if that man is one's husband.

This principle is easily seen in certain conflict situations. If a woman came to you and said her husband wanted her to participate in a bank robbery and she was torn between her loyalty to her husband and to God, the correct advice is pretty clear. You might sympathize with her conflict, but because God has said, "Thou shalt not steal," you could, without hesitation, show her that her loyalty to God supersedes her loyalty to her husband. This is an extreme example, but I use it to illustrate that there are times when the resolution of a conflict of loyalties is relatively simple.

However, in areas where God's Word is more difficult to discern, it is more common to feel torn. Your situation is an example of this. In circumstances as complex as those you describe, I would exercise great caution.

First, as I have already said, you are upset over a

problem that may not even exist, or if it does, it may have little or no effect on your ministry.

Second, I am not clear about what you view your personal responsibility to be. Do you think that you should notify both the insurance company and your church that your husband *may* have a disease that *may* affect his ministry? What would be the purpose of doing so? You are not obligated before God to disclose a "maybe" to anyone. If your husband has a visible effect, such as a tremor, and someone directly asks you its cause, then, of course, you must not lie. You could respond by saying, "We do not yet know what is causing that, but we have been encouraged by the doctor to look into it."

Scripture makes it clear that we are to be truthful at all times, but we are also told to be "slow to speak" (James 1:19) and not to "speak against one another" (4:11 NASB). Amy Carmichael wrote about a sieve she used to process her words through prior to speaking. It consisted of three questions: Is it true? Is it kind? Is it necessary? I have found these questions to be very helpful in determining whether to speak about something. Many things may be true or kind but by no means necessary for us to say.

Last, emotional discomfort or conflict over a course of action does not always mean it is wrong. Certainly the Holy Spirit can speak to us in that way, but it must always be checked against God's Word. In vague circumstances, such as the ones you describe, the first priority is to find greater clarity. Get some answers first, then deal with the loyalty issue. If indeed your husband is diagnosed as ill and he asks you to cover for him or lie when asked directly, then the question of loyalty becomes very real. At that point I would confront him with what you perceive to be disobedience to God's Word and your own unwillingness to disobey God. Then ask him to pray *with* you regarding this matter. Give him the time and opportunity to choose a different course.

If after *repeated* attempts, your husband still asks you to lie, then and only then would you be forced to choose between God and man. Given your many years together, as well as your effective ministry, it is unlikely that you will come to this place. I would encourage you rather to use this difficult time in which you face the unknown to support each other.

You must both be experiencing difficult and frightening feelings. Yet you seem isolated from each other and the body. At this stage this isolation concerns me much more than the loyalty issue. Talk with your husband; pray with your husband, continually asking God for his direction and his wisdom. God knows your future: "All the days ordained for [you] were written in [God's] book" (Ps. 139:16). He has not left you alone. He has given you and your husband to each other and planted you in the midst of part of his family. And I believe that he has equipped some of that family to support and encourage you as you walk through this difficult time. Use the resources that God has given you, and in your doing so, "May the God of hope fill you with all joy and peace as you trust in him, so that you may overflow with hope by the power of the Holy Spirit" (Rom. 15:13).

Dear Diane,

I am stuck. Throughout my life I have gotten along well with people. I enjoy relationships and have generally felt confident in nurturing and maintaining them—that is, until now.

We are in our first pastorate. The congregation has been reserved toward me. I am a professional woman, but I stopped working outside the home when our first child was born. Both before and after her birth, I have sought to do my share in the church.

Since the beginning of our service here, one woman has given me a very difficult time. She is brash, loud, and aggressive. She has a reputation for picking apart every pastor's wife who has been here.

We have had several clashes. On two occasions we have sat down with our husbands to work it out. She does not listen, and she makes unfounded accusations. On one occasion I asked her forgiveness though she had twisted the facts unbelievably. However, nothing has changed.

When she wants to impress someone, she changes completely. She is courteous and full of "spiritual" talk. I do not know how to handle this. I want to glorify God, but whatever I do or do not do, I am attacked. Please help!

In his love,
Nancy

CHAPTER 5

Why Does This Woman
Make Trouble for Me?

Proverbs 18:13 says, "He who answers before listening—that is his folly and his shame." After reading your letter several times, I concluded that I would be in danger of reaping some folly and shame unless I asked you some questions before venturing an answer.

Were we to sit down together and discuss your problem, the direction of that discussion would be dictated by your responses to my questions. Since we do not have the opportunity for this type of interchange, I would like to proceed by posing several questions and responding to each as though you have answered them affirmatively. I hope this will help you to understand some possible sources for this woman's antagonism, enable you to see how her behavior is affecting you, and give you ways to deal effectively with this problem.

You have described an individual who is frustrating and hard to get along with. When I meet such a person, my first response is to wonder why: What purpose does her behavior serve? What events in her life helped mold her this way? Why might she desire to define herself as the one who "gives the pastor's wife a hard time"?

The ideal solution would be to spend some time with the woman in an attempt to come to some understanding of the dynamics involved, but since this is not feasible, let me offer some answers based on my experience with people in general and with church problems in particular.

One possible reason for this woman's behavior is that she defines her role in the church in such a way that "the pastor's wife" infringes on her territory. Perhaps she sees herself as the one to whom people go when they have a problem, or the one to whom they direct their "spiritual" questions. They may not relate to her at all in these ways, but if she believes they do or would if given the opportunity, your very presence becomes a threat. It might be beneficial to explore her role in your church, real or imagined, to see if this is so. If it is, perhaps there are other ways she can be made to feel of value to the church or specifically helpful to you and/or your husband. Whatever difficulties she has in relating to others, God has blessed her with gifts to be used for the body. She may be frustrated and angry because she has not been given the opportunity to use those gifts.

A second explanation for her behavior might lie in her relationship to your husband and to previous pastors. Not infrequently, people who have difficulties with the minister—who disagree with him or feel unimportant to him—are unable to talk with him about these feelings. They may hold back because of fear of being rejected, or they may have a pattern of problems relative to authority figures, or they may be unaware of the source of their negative feelings. Whatever the reason, people in these circumstances will often attack the minister's wife or attempt to discredit her. It is basically a variation on the theme of the woman who keeps calling the pastor's wife to say, "I don't want to bother your husband, so I'll just let you know that he really shouldn't . . ."

If this description fits the woman you are writing about, it may be insightful to gain some understanding of her relationships with previous pastors as opposed to focusing on their wives.

A third possible reason for this woman's behavior, also not uncommon, is that through a hidden process a church picks a scapegoat who acts as the funnel for all the church's criticism. When this occurs, others rarely act hostile or speak negatively of the pastor and/or his wife, but instead they channel negative feelings into a spokesperson. This phenomenon is not unlike what is encountered in family therapy. When a family comes for help, there is always an individual who is "the problem," who is labeled "crazy," "sick," "rebellious," or some other equivalent. The plea of the family is that if this person is cured, everything will be fine. But this is not so, because the person acts as the funnel for all the hostilities and problems in the family. If indeed he does get better, the family structure will crumble. The only way to avoid that is for all members to learn healthy, honest communication. Again, this kind of family problem can often happen within the church family, and unless both the individual and the body are dealt with, nothing will change. It is conceivable that you and your husband walked into a pattern established many years ago by a pastor unable to deal with criticism.

Finally, you mention your past experience as a

professional and your newness in the congregation. A young professional woman entering a rural church poses an immediate threat to many parishioners, especially women. Some will be intimidated, others will assume you think you know it all, and yet others will be sure you will never like and/or understand them. This woman may simply be one of those. The reserve you have sensed in the congregation may reflect some of these feelings. It is difficult to wait months or sometimes years for a community to open itself up to us and allow us to serve it to our full capacity.

Whenever we are confronted with someone who is hard to get along with, we need to try, creatively and energetically, to understand him or her. We may not always be successful, but even a small amount of light on a subject changes our perspective. Perhaps you and your husband could talk with an elder who has been in the church for a long time, and, using the above possibilities plus some of your own, could get a better handle on why this woman comes across as she does. In doing this, look for *patterns* in her behavior. You make no mention of the content of your "run-ins," but maybe there is a theme going through them. Do these troubled times seem to stem from jealousy? Does she attack when something has caused her to look or feel inadequate? Must she always be right in relationship to authority figures? If so, her difficulty is not so much with who you are but with the position you hold.

Whatever the reason for her behavior and however much insight you acquire, at bottom you are faced with the hardship of responding to someone who is handling her feelings inadequately and acting inappropriately. She presents herself in an abrasive way that elicits frustration, anger, and feelings of being caught in a dilemma. How do you handle such a person?

It is of primary importance to recognize the feelings that such an individual causes in others such as yourself. The initial and perhaps the strongest reaction is one of anger. We feel angry at that person's treatment of us, angry at the control he or she has over us, and angry that he or she somehow manages to make us look like the bad one. We, as Christians, often have difficulty admitting such feelings, particularly toward an individual we are expected to spiritually nurture. Though you never say it, I sense from your letter that you are angry, and understandably so. The place to begin is with that anger, which is a normal response to such a frustrating situation.

Anger is often expressed inappropriately and destructively. However, this need not be so. If we learn not to fear it, anger can be not only controlled but also used to change a situation constructively. We must begin with understanding what we are angry about. Sometimes the reason for our anger is very clear, but when it is not, it is helpful to finish the incomplete sentence, "I am angry because . . ." with whatever comes to mind, as many times as possible. Once we focus on what is making us angry, then we can stand back to see if our perspective needs adjusting.

We must ask questions such as: Do I always react angrily to suggestions and/or criticisms? Am I angry at the same juncture in other relationships? For example, do I get angry whenever I feel less preferred than another? Am I expressing anger at another situation by using this relationship as an outlet?

Following this process, we need to ask how our anger is showing. It always comes through, whether we intend it to or not. Anger may show in one's face, one's tone of voice, one's body language, or sometimes even in one's trying too hard to please.

The next step is to decide how you want your anger to show. It is evident from your letter that you want to please God and to be effective in your situation. Let me offer a few guidelines, keeping in mind that I know nothing of your previous interaction.

First, when a relationship keeps coming up against a brick wall, further discussion should involve a third party. I suggest either an elder or an older woman in whom you both would have confidence. Avoid bringing in your husband, because the more she perceives him to be in alliance with you, the less effective his ministry in her life will be. It would be wise to use someone with a long history in the church, for he or she will offer a helpful perspective.

The second guideline goes without saying, but I will say it anyway because its importance is immeasurable. Any meeting with this woman must be preceded by much prayer and careful self-examination before God. The purpose of the meeting is not to prove her wrong and yourself right. Its purpose is to achieve unity. Regardless of its outcome, you are admonished to love her and forgive her when she wrongs you. This is a well-known truth, but it is difficult to practice!

The third guideline is that you need to assume some control over the situation. It sounds like you have been on the defensive and apologetic end of these conversations, and it is time to reverse that. You do not want to attack her, certainly, but there is no need to open yourself up to her attack. You must clearly state your case. For example:

> I sense that you are having difficulty accepting me in my role as the pastor's wife and that you are finding fault with many of the things I do and say. I am

saddened by this and have found myself angry with you when I have felt unjustly accused. Because we have not, on previous occasions, been able to resolve this problem, I want us to establish some guidelines for future interactions. This is important to me, because I do not want our difficulty to be disruptive to the body in any way. I believe God has called me to be here alongside my husband, and I want to love and serve you and all members of the community as best I can.

Certainly I will make some mistakes, and I would like to know about them in a loving, constructive way. When I am accused and discredited, I do not find that helpful. Would you support me in my role here by coming to me in the presence of _____ (elder or older woman you have chosen), and lovingly offer suggestions you have prayed over thoughtfully? Though I am sure we will not always agree, I will listen to your suggestions and pray together with you and _____ (elder). I am sure that as we do this, God will work in us and teach us to walk in unity together. If you will do this in the manner I have described, you will be of great help to me, and we will be on our way to establishing a mutually rewarding relationship.

You will find your anger somewhat dissipated if you speak to her this way, for you will not feel so stuck and frustrated. Having done it, you must then lovingly and firmly hold her to your guidelines. Do not apologize for something you have not done. If she continues to attack and discredit you, then prayerfully go to your board of elders, because she is clearly being disruptive of the body and she then becomes a candidate for church discipline.

Finally, the battle is fought before God. Only he can give you the grace to love the unlovely, to be gracious to those who are rude, and to handle in wisdom those who attack you. There will always be someone who does not like you and who does not even want to try. Loving such a person means both serving her and holding her to the utmost. Treat her graciously and gently, for she obviously is crippled in her relationships with others. But you must also admonish and encourage her to act in a way that unites the body of which she is a part. It is a difficult balance, but I am confident that God will fill you with his graciousness and wisdom and enable you to find this balance.

Dear Diane,

What I am experiencing is not unique, but I feel very much alone. My husband is a successful pastor, and we have a good marriage. My difficulty is physical; the doctors call it a hormone imbalance. For a few days each month I end up in bed. My husband understands, for he has listened to several doctors with me.

The difficulty lies in the way my husband handles this issue with the congregation. Many understand and accept the situation, and, in fact, have cared for me lovingly. However, there are others who always ask questions and cause my husband and children great awkwardness. He does not know how to deal with this or what to say. I will often force myself out of bed to protect my family, but with dire consequences for me.

I do not want to hinder his ministry. Anything you can suggest for us would be appreciated.

In Christ,
Marilee

CHAPTER 6
What Can I Do About Premenstrual Syndrome?

You have described some painful and difficult problems that may be related to a controversial disorder known as Premenstrual Syndrome (PMS). Health professionals have debated about the nature of this condition for years, and while it is generally agreed that PMS exists, there continues to be little consensus about its cause and treatment. We have only just begun to listen to women regarding what they experience during their menstrual cycles. The issue is a complex one from a medical, psychological, and social standpoint.

DEFINING THE PROBLEM

It is generally agreed that the distinguishing features of PMS surround the cyclical nature and timing of symptoms. Typically, symptoms begin one to ten days before menstruation and continue until after the onset of menses. Another common pattern is for symptoms to begin just after ovulation and to continue until near the end of the menstrual period. Most patterns are followed by a symptom-free phase of at least one week.

It is important to distinguish PMS from dysmenorrhea, or painful menstruation. PMS occurs before menstruation and can be described in terms of three clusters of symptoms. The pain cluster includes symptoms such as cramps, headache, backache, and muscle spasms. The psychological group of symptoms includes tension, irritability, depression, anxiety, and mood swings. The edema (swelling) aspect of PMS includes such symptoms as breast tenderness, weight gain, and swollen joints. Other symptoms of PMS that occur less frequently include food cravings, clumsiness, acne, dizziness, nausea, fatigue, insomnia, changes in sex drive, and difficulty concentrating.

It is estimated that PMS affects 70 to 90 percent of women at some time during their childbearing years. It is most common among women in their twenties and thirties. Some women first experience PMS following pregnancy or after discontinuing birth control pills.

There are many different theories about the causes of PMS; none are universally agreed upon, and none seem to be true for all women with premenstrual symptoms. Explanations include estrogen excess, progesterone deficiency, hypoglycemia, allergy, hormones, fluid retention, vitamin deficiency, and psychological stress.

The diagnosis of PMS is, to some extent, a subjective one. It is best arrived at by careful observation of one's own symptoms and frank discussion with a concerned gynecologist.

The negative connotation that has surrounded symptoms like depression and anxiety can complicate a woman's search for answers. Deciding whether or not one does have PMS and then finding the proper treatment is a process that can take months. It starts with the recognition and validation that these symptoms are part of the menstrual cycle. It is useful to keep a careful daily diary of symptoms through at least one complete cycle and preferably through three menstrual periods. The first step is to make a list of the symptoms that can be charted and to assign an abbreviation for each one. Next, make a calendar and enter the appropriate abbreviation for each symptom on every day that it appears. Enter an "M" for each day of the menstrual flow. In most cases, PMS symptoms will appear one to ten days before menstruation. This is generally followed by a symptom-free period of a week or more.

The charting of symptoms provides an understanding of how one's particular symptoms relate to the menstrual cycle and helps the woman and her physician to arrive at a diagnosis of PMS. Often, just knowing that such symptoms are real, definable, and chartable has significant therapeutic value. Understanding and defining the existence of a problem allows us to realistically confront the problem and to channel our energies toward its amelioration. It bears repeating that the lack of specificity and the controversy surrounding PMS have added to the burden of those women who experience it. The recognition that there may be predictable "bad days" when we are hampered by valid physical and psychological symptoms can allow us to plan around these times to the extent to which it is possible. Family members can be alerted to those times when we might need extra help and understanding from them. This is not to suggest that we are to be treated with kid gloves at these times or that we expect others to excuse any behavior that may be linked to PMS. Greater tolerance and compassion—both for ourselves and from others who understand and love us is, however, of tremendous importance.

THINGS THAT MAY HELP

After charting your symptoms, or even before doing so, consult your physician. He or she will help diagnose the problem and guide you in its treatment.

Many cases of PMS have been controlled successfully through dietary changes. Cutting down on sodium reduces water retention; cutting back on sugar and caffeine may help to alleviate tension and irritability.

Exercise can be helpful in reducing depression, anxiety, tension, and fatigue. If you do not have a planned exercise program, a daily brisk walk is a good way to begin.

Many women have found relief by taking supplements of Vitamin B_6. Some physicians recommend B_6 supplements of 50 to 200 milligrams per day to relieve irritability, fatigue, and depression. However, B_6 has been reported to be toxic in high doses and should be used with caution.

Some nonprescription medications often recommended by physicians for treating PMS are acetaminophen for pain relief; pyrilamine maleate for relief of irritability and cramps; and pamabrom for relief of general PMS symptoms. But these medications generally have not been shown to provide consistent relief.

Of the prescription medications, progesterone is the most widely publicized. However, it has not yet been approved by the Federal Drug Administration for the treatment of PMS, and its effectiveness has not been scientifically demonstrated.

Some combination of the above treatments will probably be of benefit to most women who experience PMS. Your doctor can help you in determining which of these are helpful for you personally.

SOME THOUGHTS ABOUT YOUR OWN STRUGGLE

From the tone of your letter it is obvious that you desire to please God and to be an asset to your husband. I am concerned, however, that you may see yourself as a hindrance to your husband due to your struggles. I would like to offer some suggestions pertaining to that possibility.

First, when God in his sovereignty created women, he did so knowing the end from the beginning. In his creation of us, his sovereignty was not only over our assets but also over our liabilities. When God made you the woman that you are, he knew who your husband would be, what your ministry would be, and where he would lead you. Knowing all of this, he allowed problems with your menstrual cycle to be part of that package. Gifts or assets are easier to accept than limitations, particularly when our desire is to serve God and minister to others, but it is important to learn to accept both as coming from God. As we do accept both assets and limitations as coming from God, we grow in our faith rather than continually struggling with the Potter and asking, "Why did you make me like this?" (Rom. 9:20).

Second, ask yourself, "How can God use my struggle, my limitations, in his service?" Obviously, we are not speaking here of limitations in the sense of sinful behavior that requires repentance but rather of aspects of our makeup over which we have limited control. In thinking about how God can use our struggles, 2 Corinthians 1:3—4 comes to mind: "Praise be to . . . the

61

Father of compassion and the God of all comfort, who comforts us in all our troubles, so that we can comfort those in any trouble with the comfort we ourselves have received from God." As you seek comfort in Christ in the midst of frustration, misunderstanding, and perhaps misjudgment from others, he will encourage you with a comfort you can share. He will perhaps use you to minister to others more gently or compassionately than you might otherwise have done. Ask God to show you specifically who these people are. They might not experience any difficulty with PMS as you do, but theirs may be a similar struggle in terms of frustration or misunderstanding. Actively look for those to whom you can minister *because* of your difficulties rather than in spite of them.

You may also wish to ask yourself whether your experiences and unique perspective may help you to minister to or aid your husband in new ways. Adversities alter our viewpoints; how we are changed depends on our response to them. Our own struggles can bring bitterness, anger, and self-pity, or they can broaden our horizons and enlarge our capacity for compassion. Might you be able to minister more effectively to your husband during his own times of frustration and misunderstanding? Can you help him to see Mr. and Mrs. X's difficulties in a new light because of your expanded outlook?

With respect to the tensions in your own family, you may be able to help your husband and children formulate an approach to your symptoms that might ease their own discomfort. For example, in response to those who ask, "Is she sick again?" your family might reply, "Yes, and we greatly appreciate your prayers during this time. It saddens her not to be here with us." Another approach to such awkward questions might be for your husband to share his own experience and discernment regarding your symptoms by responding along the lines of, "Yes, but I'm so grateful to God, for he has taught her to use these times to pray for me as I minister to you. It is a blessing to me as I preach that she is interceding for you and me at that moment." Thus, your husband may be able to both ease his own discomfort and minister to others by sharing his own broadened perspective.

We all encounter times when we are misunderstood and perhaps misjudged by others. Your trials with PMS cause you to be especially vulnerable in this regard, as the symptoms which you experience are not tangible to others in the way that physical difficulties may be. Those who have never experienced any hint of premenstrual problems might find it hard to conceptualize exactly what you are suffering. Paradoxically, those women who have experienced mild premenstrual symptoms may be even less understanding. They are uncomfortable, too, but they continue with their lives. These women (and their husbands) may think that they know what you are experiencing and make judgments based on these assumptions. In many respects, these people require more enlightenment than those who have no experience with the problem at all.

In confronting all of this, the key is for you and your husband to take the problem and all the difficulties it generates to God in prayer. How can he use this to honor his name and further his ministry? The tendency is to say, "If only I didn't have this problem, then I could. . . ." Approach it from the other side: How can God use this difficulty to make us better equipped as his servants? How can he use this to minister to the people in our congregation?

Second Corinthians 4:7–10 tells us that we have this treasure in earthen vessels ("jars of clay," NIV) for a purpose. The purpose is not to hinder God's work, as we so often fear, but rather that the greatness of the power may be seen to be from God and not from ourselves. You and your husband are experiencing this so that the life of Jesus may be manifested in and through you to the people you so lovingly and willingly serve.

May God bless you and your husband as you honor him in your struggle.

Dear Diane,

I am a pastor's wife, and I believe that I am to be a partner in ministry with my husband. However, the women in our congregation are distant and cold to me. I feel alienated from them and therefore unable to participate fully in the life of the church. I have been successful in areas outside home and church. Do you think I am a threat to the women?

My husband is very supportive, and I am grateful. I would also like some support and openness from the women. Can you recommend how I might find acceptance from these women?

Sincerely,
Teresa

CHAPTER 7

Why Do Women in the Church Keep Their Distance From Me?

Your letter reflects not only perplexity but feelings of loneliness as well. Apparently, you have engaged in considerable self-analysis to make certain that you have not added to the problem by alienating others. Let's proceed by considering some circumstances that are likely to produce a sense of isolation. Then we will take a look at what our response might be when we find ourselves in such a situation.

Loneliness that results from an inability to have effective relationships with others is something over which, in the power of Christ, we have control. The kind of isolation to which you refer, however, appears circumstantial and is thus in somewhat of a different category. A single woman on an isolated mission field, a woman in a leadership position, or a widow, will all experience loneliness by virtue of their position in life. In counseling many pastors and their wives I often hear comments such as: "We don't know where to go for friends" and "People either shy away from us or play up to us, and we can't establish normal friendships." Hardly a seminar passes in which a similar comment does not arise. Your sense of alienation is not peculiar to you; it is a difficulty you share with many other women in your position.

Why is this? I believe that the answer lies largely in the fact that many women in the congregation see you as a role and not as a person. You are not Jane or Sally; you are the pastor's wife. Depending on the church and its history, this role is surrounded by a certain set of expectations. People are often caught between wanting you to be perfect and hoping that they will find a flaw so that they can feel more comfortable around you. You can clearly see this ambivalence in the public's response to political figures. They look hard for some dirt they can throw around, but when they do find it they are furious with the person for failing to meet their expectations.

The conflict between others' expectations of you and your ability to meet them is often complicated by the setting of the church. Many find it difficult to adjust to a small town or rural congregation where certain unspoken rules and methods govern the lives of those there. The pastor's wife is an outsider and is often considered a foreigner. One woman spoke of the difficulties of moving to a rural church after having had a successful professional career. She found herself in a congregation where no woman had ever worked outside the home. She felt terribly alienated by the judgments and assumptions of church members. Establishing relationships with the women proved slow and difficult due to the conclusions they drew from her having had a career.

Though pastors also deal with role-related struggles, their wives usually have more difficulty in this area. Part of the reason for this difficulty is the ambiguity of your position. Your husband has a job description that both he and the church have decided he can fill satisfactorily. You must also fill a job description, but one that is unstated by the church and unclear to you. You are left guessing and are accepted according to your ability to figure out the church's expectations and succeed in meeting them.

It is impossible to say what is causing your particular sense of alienation. We must always be open before God to the possibility that we are inadvertently contributing to another's distance from us. However, if there is no obvious indication that this is so, we must proceed to discover how to overcome the barrier.

Needless to say, handling this situation appropriately has a lot to do with your attitude and behavior. I have a specific suggestion that has been followed successfully by others in similar circumstances. It may be beneficial for you to choose two or three women who are considered leaders by the others (your husband's input here would be helpful). Tell them you have a concern for the church and particularly for the women of the church. Ask them, based on their own experience with other pastor's wives, how they feel you might best be able to serve the women in the congregation. Obviously, your service would be unique, as it would be based on your gifts and personality, but perhaps these women would be in a position to offer some suggestions and to make more clear to you the needs and expectations you are facing.

This being done, I believe your task is best accomplished by walking among these women as a servant. Peter's exhortation to the elders (1 Peter 5:1—3) is applicable to all in leadership positions. Peter challenges us to shepherd God's people willingly and eagerly, always proving to be an example in our walk.

The type of example you are is the key to whether you will find yourself in a receptive, like-minded congregation or in a rejecting, dissimilar one. You are there as a servant to your sisters in Christ. Certainly they are also there as your servants. However, your major task is to serve as an example to them. If you focus on their lack of response, you risk becoming filled with bitterness and pain, and you will fail to serve willingly and eagerly.

You ask what you can do in order to be accepted. I do not know. Acceptance is something we all want and enjoy, but it is not to be our goal. The Shepherd whom we follow was not accepted; people rejected him. He knew the feeling of aloneness. He lived with constant and pressing crowds, irregular hours of work and sleep, no settled home, and always knowing that his was a mission of rejection.

We are not to pursue acceptance *or* rejection but rather strive to be like him whatever response we face. Our concern must not be others' response to us but rather our walk before them. Others may be intimidated by our competence, or they may reject us because of our failures. Paul exhorts us: ". . . live a life worthy of the calling you have received. Be completely humble and gentle; be patient, bearing with one another in love. Make every effort to keep the unity of the Spirit through the bond of peace" (Eph. 4:1–3).

We are to walk as Christ walked. He walked humbly and "did not consider equality with God something to be grasped" (Phil. 2:6). We are not to draw attention to our competencies or to our successes. Jesus was kind to those who were fearful or uncomfortable in his presence, always reaching out to draw them to himself. He continued to love those who forsook him, and he was patient with their lack of response. He should have been honored, given due respect, and accepted as God's Son, yet he restrained himself and did not demand these rights. He walked diligently, constantly working to build up the body.

If we walk in Christ's way, we will find a true unity with some. A friendship blessed by common goals and that oneness that the Spirit of God brings is a joy indeed. I pray that you will find such a friend. Indeed, it sounds as if you might be married to one! Continue to enjoy your husband's friendship and support. Perhaps another friend will come along in a co-worker, a sister in Christ. In the meantime, as you minister in this time of apparent isolation, continually ask yourself: "How can I love this one? How can I bring unity to this body? How can I minister to this one's needs?" Ministering to others will not eliminate your loneliness; it will not even always remove the pain that loneliness brings. It will, however, keep your focus where it must be if your ministry is to glorify God and contribute to the unity of the body. Your example will cause other women to respond to you and to each other, encouraging the body to "grow and build itself up in love, as each part does its work" (Eph. 4:16).

Dear Diane,

My husband is a pastor, and we have several children. Two of the children are adults. My husband thinks that they respect him, but they really don't. They think that they can do whatever they want in our home. They do everything imaginable—use drugs, violate the law, and engage in free sex.

If we say anything, they threaten to leave and say we don't love them. We know we can win them only with love and a Christ-like attitude. We are uncertain how to do so. We are afraid of the church's reaction if we lose our children.

Sincerely,
Eunice

CHAPTER 8
What Can We Do With Rebellious Older Children?

Raising children becomes increasingly difficult as they grow older. You are in an upsetting and frustrating situation, but perhaps a review of some of the important aspects of parenting will alter your perspective somewhat.

You say in your letter that "we . . . can win them only with love and a Christ-like attitude." That is certainly a true statement, but I believe we need to define our terms more clearly. What do we mean when we speak of loving our children? What is a Christ-like attitude in a parent?

Truly loving our children means always holding them to the highest; always expecting and encouraging the best in them. Sometimes that is done with great gentleness and patience as we tend to their wounds or when we swallow our impatient words after they repeat the same mistake. At other times we hold them to the highest with discipline or correction. Clearly, parents who love their toddlers will discipline them firmly to prevent them from going into the street.

Love is not without form. Love has limits, and it even places demands on loved ones. Love in marriage, for example, demands exclusivity. God's love demands obedience. He says, "If anyone loves me, he will obey my teaching" (John 14:23) and "Be perfect . . . as your heavenly Father is perfect" (Matt. 5:48). We must not let the world squeeze us into its mold.

The world says that if someone loves me that person will demonstrate love by pleasing me. If I am not pleased, I am not loved. There is a nugget of truth in that. The wife who loves her husband will endeavor to please him. However, love is guided by certain standards. A loving wife will not break the law for her husband. That is because love is not determined by the recipient (or the giver) but by God, who has clearly defined love in action. I counseled a woman many years ago whose husband had been sexually abusing their daughter. She had told no one because her husband had told her repeatedly, "If you love me, you won't turn me in." This is far removed from God's definition of love.

Many people today are saying that discipline of children will kill creativity. Some say that limits in marriage are not evidence of love; that true love allows the loved one to go and be with whomever he/she wants. Your children are saying much the same thing to you. "Mom and Dad, if you really loved us, you would let us do whatever we want, and the fact that you try to stop us shows how lacking in love you really are."

Loving our children in a Christ-like way means that we must firmly hold to God's guidelines. We are not to be guided by what our children want or even by what they think they need. Our method for training is to be found in how God trains and directs us. He does so with a love that demands obedience. He loves us with a patience that never forgets that we are dust, yet he never compromises his standards for us.

Two illustrations of this balance come to mind. The first is found in Luke 18:18—25. This is the story of the rich young ruler who questioned Christ about how he might obtain eternal life. He was a man who, in outward appearance, was very righteous, yet Christ's response was to dig deeper and point to where this man failed before God. Christ continually held others to the highest. This man responded negatively; he chose not to follow Christ. And Jesus' response was to let him go. He did not condemn him or berate him, but he did part ways with him.

The second illustration is in Hebrews 4:15—16, where we are told that we have Christ as our High Priest. He sympathizes with our weaknesses, yet though he was tempted, he did not sin. There is that balance again. God never forgets our frailties, but he holds us to obedience, for we are to walk as Christ walked. We must show this balance in our relationships with each other, whether it be husband-wife, parent-child, or any other. It is so easy to go to extremes. We can work so hard on loving that we fail to hold another to obedience. On the other hand, we can be so involved in demanding obedience that we forget that the one with whom we are dealing is dust.

You and your husband have let your children define how you should love them. They are manipulating you with guilt to get what they want. It is not acceptable for them to do as they please in your home. Your home is a stage, given to you by God for the purpose of glorifying him. Their behavior and disrespect dishonor God. They will not change, for there is no reason why they should—they can stay home and do as they please without fear of consequences.

I suggest that, first, you and your husband talk at length together. You said in your letter that your children do not really respect their father, though he thinks they do. You need to confront your husband with this situation, lovingly and gently, as well as with your own feelings. Together you must decide what your home stands for and what it is to demonstrate to those around you. Then you need to decide how the two of you *together* will handle behaviors and attitudes that fight against your goals. You will need to stand firm in some areas but compromise in others. Decide what you will do in case your children choose to utterly defy what you set before them. Though I believe it is rare, there is a place in some parent/adult-child relationships where the parents have to say: "We have taught you what we believe to be right before God, and you have refused to honor that in our home. If you choose to live in defiance of these standards, which we believe cannot be compromised, then you will have to live elsewhere." It is a terrible heartbreak when this happens, and certainly it occurs only after much effort (and many tears) toward a better resolution, but sometimes it must be done. Just as Christ let the young ruler go, sometimes we must let our children go.

I recently counseled a couple in a situation similar to yours. The father made an appropriate observation: "I guess our standards are meaningless unless we are willing to stand by them all the way, even if it means parting ways with our daughter." This is very true, and it means two things: (1) Do not make arbitrary or unimportant rules. Make a few carefully chosen rules. (2) Only make rules that you are willing to part ways over. For example, you do not want to kick your children out because they fail to wash the dishes. You may, however, want to tell them that if they break the law in your home, they must leave.

You cannot make your adult children obey you. You cannot hide them from your congregation or from the townspeople. Probably more people are aware of your situation than you think. The problem is not "How can we make our children behave differently?" but "How can we handle their defiance in a way that glorifies God?" If you and your husband do not work on this issue together, then you are giving a message to those around you and, more sadly, to your younger children that this behavior is acceptable. Your message is that their actions are worth making a few noises about and verbalizing disagreement with, but that you will still allow it to occur. That is not a demonstration of the balance we have discussed. It is the equivalent of saying to a toddler, "I wish you wouldn't go into the street, but if you insist, I guess there is nothing I can do about it."

One final word comes from the apostle Paul in his first letter to Timothy. Paul writes that the one who oversees or shepherds others must "manage his own family well and see that his children obey him with proper respect. (If anyone does not know how to manage his own family, how can he take care of God's church?)" (3:4—5). Your children will not be likely to respect either you or your husband unless you walk in obedience to the Word that you teach. Your home is a place where the love of God is to be evident in your patience, gentleness, and understanding; but it is also a place to glorify God by your obedience to the standard to which he has called you. May God bless you and your husband as you strive to find and maintain this balance.

Dear Diane,

I would like some straight talk about the church's support—primarily financial—of the pastor and his family.

Here is my situation. Our church is experiencing budget difficulties. At the annual meeting a woman I have counseled through a depression stood up and asked why the pastor was getting a raise if the church was having trouble meeting its budget. The raise in question was only cost-of-living and was finally approved. Her attitude, however, and that of others who agreed, stung terribly.

We pastor a well-to-do congregation, but most of the people do not tithe. I feel that their attitude toward my husband's salary indicates that we are not valued by the church. I feel betrayed.

What can I do about my feelings? What is appropriate for us to say regarding our support? Should we simply smile and say nothing?

I suspect many ministry couples struggle with this. Can you give us any clear answers?

Thank you.

In Christ,
Emily

CHAPTER 9

How Can We Handle a Lack of Support—Financial and Otherwise?

The love of money is a root of all kinds of evil" (1 Tim. 6:10). Many congregations take Paul's warning to heart when it pertains to the minister's salary—that is, if the love of money is the root of evil, they want to ensure that their minister does not have too much.

The issue of financial remuneration poses special problems for ministers and their wives. It is an area that surfaces repeatedly in my work with clergymen, who often are ill-prepared to deal with such matters.

I would like to approach this complex problem from two standpoints. First, we need to understand the issue from a practical and spiritual perspective. Second, we must consider the interpersonal complexities that are a part of every helping relationship.

In most professional settings the server determines his/her fee based upon his/her own assessment of its value. The client then decides whether or not to

engage the services of a professional; he is generally
not, however, in a position of dictating the financial
worth of these services. Can you imagine being treated
by a doctor and telling him or her that you thought the
visit was worth about five dollars and that is what you
will pay? He would be at your mercy. He might
disagree and feel that he had worked very hard, but
you would have the power to set the fee. Perhaps you
chose five dollars because you genuinely believed that
that was his worth, but you may have done so because
you were stingy, were on a low budget that week, did
not like him, or just felt that he made enough money
already. Obviously, the doctor's position would be an
awkward and insecure one—very much like the one
you have described.

Scripture makes it clear that the church should be
generous to its laborers. We are told in 1 Timothy
5:17: "The elders who direct the affairs of the church
well are worthy of double honor, especially those
whose work is preaching and teaching." Though
speaking of a different principle, Paul states the same
thing in 1 Corinthians 9:11: "If we have sown spiritual
seed among you, is it too much if we reap a material
harvest from you?" Our pastors are to be given *double*
honor in the form of material support and are to be
recognized as worthy of this esteem. Some churches
live out this principle beautifully, but some do not.

Many ministers are hesitant to preach about
money for fear that they will be seen as requesting
more for themselves. Paul, however, did not hesitate to
preach about and discuss finances with the church at
Corinth, and contemporary ministers may follow his
example.

I offer the following recommendations with great
caution, as Scripture never gives priority to the material needs of God's servants. However, when a church

repeatedly resists giving their pastor a raise (in essence, negating his worth to them), I would encourage that minister to take the following steps.

First, he must examine himself. Are he and his wife serving their people generously and lovingly, or are they angry and bitter for not being rendered their due? True service does not look for reward, and our heart's attitude must reflect this. If, however, a pastor's full efforts are truly hindered by a congregation's lack of financial support, he must feel free to discuss this with his church.

The second step is for the minister to go lovingly to the elders, session, or board and present the problem. I would suggest he lay out before them what Paul says in 1 Timothy and 1 Corinthians, balanced with what Scripture says about serving others. This must not be done out of resentment but out of a true servant heart. Then their prayerful advice should be sought: "What should we do? This situation in the church is wrong, and we are suffering because of it. Will you pray with us regarding the next step? Should I as a pastor go to the people? Should you as elders present this issue to the congregation?" God could use these steps when taken cautiously and lovingly to instruct a church in giving double honor to those who serve them, and what blessings such a congregation would reap!

The second aspect of the problem involves understanding the emotional dynamics of those you serve. As you open up your life and home, you will serve all varieties and shapes of humanity. Many will bless you, endear themselves to you, and bring you joy. Some will not. Some, like the nine lepers in Luke 17, will go on their way with no thought for you, no word of gratitude. Having reaped the benefit of your service to them, they will show no thankfulness. There is, however, an even more puzzling type of person, perhaps similar to the woman mentioned in your letter. Often, this will be the very one to whom you have gone in the middle of the night; the one with whom you have sat when every bone in your body was tired and when other things and people were demanding your attention. This person can be the one who not only utters no word of gratitude but who stands against you in your time of need. Why? How can she do such a thing?

The answer lies in the dynamics of the relationship. When you have helped someone through a depression such as the one you described, you have entered a counseling relationship with that person. That relationship usually has undercurrents that are important to understand in order to deal with your own feelings. I am going to discuss two of these.

In any counseling relationship you become, in some ways, like a parent. You are there to gently care for and minister to that person in much the same way our parents did when, as children, we brought our hurts to them. The context and purpose are different, of course, but the overtones of nurturance are always present. It is needful and appropriate that these be there, for we are to serve with sympathy and compassion.

When, however, you are helping a person who has had bad parenting, your good and right actions will often elicit angry words or some form of betrayal. The person you have so lovingly helped may respond in ways that were learned in reaction to earlier hurts. These resentments tend to spill over in a counseling relationship, even when your "parenting" has been good. Such responses are often deeply ingrained and difficult to change. They will hurt you and can easily make you angry and bitter. This tends to feed the pattern, for your rejection will confirm the fear that you did not really love the person, and the cycle continues.

A similar problem occurs when people have a fear of dependency in relationships. As they open up and allow you to help them, they begin to depend on you. As their dependency increases, their ambivalence also increases, and they may experience conflicting feelings about you. The greater their need, the more they must find some fault to ensure that their image of perfection (and thus their commensurate need) is negated. Given our finiteness, they will always be successful. Again, such a response to our love and help can bring us a great deal of pain.

The understanding of these dynamics, however, can help to alleviate our feelings of resentment. To know that another person has hurt or betrayed us because of his or her own fears and that he or she is sadly locked into such a destructive behavior pattern, can enable us to continue to reach out in compassion. That person does not act this way for want of appreciation but rather because his or her love and need of us is so great!

As you struggle with the complexities of ministering to others, remember that the battle against bitterness is fought before God. Our understanding of others does not always free us from angry feelings. As I struggle in my own areas of service, God often brings me back to Ephesians 5:1–2: "Be imitators of God, therefore, as dearly loved children, and live a life of love, just as Christ loved us and gave himself up *for* us as a fragrant offering and sacrifice *to* God" (italics mine).

Christ's sacrifice was made *for* us. It was a great sacrifice made in love *for* sinful, angry, and unlovely people. However, it was made *to* God—the infinite and unchanging one. We tend to do this backwards by sacrificing *to* others and *for* God. We err when we direct our service toward those who are finite and changeable. People will fail us; they will forget to say thank you; they will hurt us. If the focus of our service is to them, we will struggle with bitterness and question our value. Our sacrifice is to be *for* others, some lovely and some not, but *to* God. Our sacrifice is to be directed toward One with whom our value is eternal and whose response of love is unchanging. This does not eliminate the pain of thanklessness, but it does lessen its effect on us, for we realize that the gratitude of those we help is not the source of our worth. This truth can bring both freedom and stability in the vicissitudes of our ministry.

May God bless you and your husband as you seek to wisely serve others in sacrifice to him.

Dear Diane,

Our denomination is undergoing theological changes, many of which my husband believes are unscriptural. Coupled with this, he has received excessive criticism for not being the outgoing, jovial type who previously pastored our church. He is a quiet, introspective man, full of concern for God's ways and Christ's body.

The upheaval seems to have immobilized him. He has withdrawn from many aspects of his ministry, particularly those requiring interpersonal skills.

How should we respond to the church's insistence that he be a certain personality type? What do I do when people come to me with complaints about him? How can I handle my feelings of anger toward the church and toward him?

He is getting some counseling, but the benefit of the session is lost as the week goes by. Why won't he help himself?

In Christ,
Arlene

CHAPTER 10

My Husband Is Depressed —What Can I Do?

Given the numerous difficulties you and your husband are facing, I do not doubt your identification with the psalmist when he spoke of being "in a dry and weary land where there is no water" (63:1). There seems to be very little refreshment in your lives in terms of caring and support from others. I hope, by looking at some of the issues raised in your letter, to provide some encouragement and insight regarding your circumstances. I want to do this by considering three areas: (1) the conflict and some alternatives; (2) your husband's depression and your response to it; and finally, (3) how to handle reactions within your church.

First, we must acknowledge and deal with the larger conflict. You and your husband are faced with struggles within your specific congregation as well as within your denomination generally. As much as possible, these two situations must be separated from one another in order to cope with either of them effectively.

The difficulties within the denomination and how they affect you do not carry the same personal overtones as do those within your particular church. It is important not to confuse the theological and the personal issues. As far as the denomination goes, you and your husband may want to sit down and consider point by point what the areas of concern are and what you believe God's Word says about them. If these are in opposition with one another, then you must prayerfully consider what God would have you to do. Should you stay within a denomination you believe is in error and continue to preach God's truth? Or will you be so hampered by external controls that you will be unable to honor his Word and therefore need to consider leaving and affiliating with a group of believers with whom you are in agreement? I cannot answer this for you, but I would encourage you both to speak and pray about this together. Handling this aspect of the problem as a team will make it easier to keep the issues clear of the emotional turmoil you are experiencing in your present church.

If you decide to stay in the denomination, you will still have the conflict in your particular church to resolve. This resolution will be more difficult because you and your husband feel attacked and misunderstood, and therefore a rational sorting out of the problem will not be easy. Handle this together, helping each other to maintain a sensible perspective. You will feel more helpful, and your husband will feel less overwhelmed.

You might begin by writing down your perceptions of the church's expectations. What jobs do they think your husband should perform? What personality traits should be evident in his relationships? What aspects of ministry do they emphasize (preaching, counseling, visitation, administration, etc.)? What aspects do they feel are less important? If you feel free to do so, you may want to ask an elder in whom you have some trust to go over these expectations and see if you have understood the church's demands correctly.

Next, you and your husband need to take a hard look at who he is and at the partnership you have. What are your goals for your ministry? What areas do you want to see emphasized? What needs do you see in the people? What gifts do you have individually and together, and how can they be used to the fullest? You must *not* lose sight of the precious fact that God has gifted all of his children—your husband being no exception. The gifts that God has given your husband to be used for God's glory are not to be buried or stomped on by others. Nor can others demand that he have gifts other than what God has given. His limitations are as much ordained by God as his abilities.

Often there is a mismatch between the pastor's gifts and the congregation's expectations. All too frequently, neither of these are made clear prior to the pastor taking the position. Evidence of a mismatch usually shows up later in vague complaints and grumblings. I have often found it helpful to sit down with the pastoral couple and help them clarify this mismatch by using the aforementioned questions. Otherwise, they may feel like miserable failures, questioning the rightness of their decision to enter the ministry and feeling very depressed. Many a man has burned out and given up his ministry because of this kind of conflict.

After you have determined whether there is a mismatch between your congregation and yourselves, you may both feel that this particular congregation is not right for you and that you are not right for them.

Such a decision *does not* mean that you have failed. It simply means that there has been a mismatch. Not all pastors have the same gifts and not all churches have the same expectations. It is important for both sides that these issues be thoroughly considered, otherwise any decision you reach will be based on the negative feelings you carry and those you sense in the congregation. If that happens, your husband will consider himself a failure, and his depression will deepen.

This brings us to the second problem, which is the depression itself. I do not know your husband, so I cannot say that his depression is purely situational; however, it is obvious that the situation is a factor. Anyone experiencing depression such as your husband's should have a complete physical exam. Many physical ailments can cause a depression that, symptomatically, is indistinguishable from a clinical depression.

It is important for you to understand that your husband's loss of energy and motivation, inability to concentrate, and feelings of hopelessness are all part of a depression. His seeming inability to act is not laziness or passivity. He is overwhelmed and in despair and probably sees no alternative but to retreat. That is one of the reasons your active involvement would be helpful. Not only will this help your anger over the circumstances, but it also will allow you to encourage him and support him so that he can begin to mobilize himself. Have you been involved in his counseling at all? If not, would he allow you to come some of the time? The more you understand his depression and the more involved you are, the more help you can be to each other.

It would be helpful to you as well to speak with the counselor, for I sense a creeping resentment toward your husband for "letting things get this far" and a fear for the future. Both are understandable, but if left untended, they have the potential to pit you and your husband against each other. It is important that you have assistance in these areas so that you are free to be the support to your husband that you so obviously want to be.

The third area you mention that causes you difficulty is the specific complaints of the people, which are directed to you instead of to your husband. Ordinarily I would say that you need to respond by directing them to your husband by saying, "My husband and I appreciate any encouragement or suggestions that you would like to offer and will prayerfully consider them. However, we do ask that you direct them to the person they concern. We find this the best way to avoid misunderstandings and hurt feelings." However, because of your husband's depression, I would not do that "across the board" at this time. Direct those who bring complaints to you to an elder with whom your husband is meeting. You may say something like this:

> This is a particularly hard time for my husband, and he very much needs your love and support. I appreciate your concern but would ask at this time that you seriously pray about your problem, and if you still feel it is necessary to present it, please go first to Mr. _____. Thank you for being so understanding.

This may be considered a bold response, but if lovingly said, it is appropriate to the need of the moment. You will be protecting your husband during a difficult time, you will be keeping yourself from hearing a myriad of complaints about which you can do nothing, and you will be lovingly guiding those in the congregation who are in need of such guidance.

There likely will be some suggestions or criticisms you will continue to direct to your husband, but God will provide the necessary wisdom for you to know which ones to redirect.

In closing, let me offer some encouragement and suggestions regarding the depression, hurt, and frustration you both feel.

First, some Christians will not acknowledge depression. They say that a Christian is one who feels happy all the time and that this has always been so for them. But we are not happy all the time; life is often ugly and harsh. People hurt us and tragedies occur that result in feelings of depression. Scripture offers hope and kindness to Christians in such a dilemma. Scripture does not condone depression nor encourage one to indulge in depression, but it does recognize its existence and offers suggestions for handling those times in our lives. (See Pss. 34:18; 40:17; 42; 2 Cor. 1:3—4; Phil. 4:6—7; 2 Tim. 1:5—7; Heb. 4:15—16.)

To help you as you try to encourage your husband, I will mention some things that I continually but gently emphasize when counseling a depressed Christian. You must be sensitive. Listen and then listen some more. When you have listened carefully and prayed much, then perhaps these points will be helpful in dealing with your husband.

Scripture makes it clear that emotions are not to rule our lives. Rather, truth must be the ruling force, and truth speaks to the mind. Our attempts to focus on making ourselves "feel better" are often misguided. Paul says in Philippians 4:4, "Rejoice in the Lord always. I will say it again: Rejoice!" That is a command. You cannot make yourself feel happy, but you can make yourself rejoice.

Happiness is usually rooted in circumstances that bring positive feelings. Rejoicing is in the Lord, who is the same yesterday, today, and forever. When Paul wrote in 2 Corinthians 4:8—9 of being troubled, perplexed, persecuted, and struck down, he did not exhibit happiness. In fact, he would have been irrational had he done so. Instead, he was rejoicing in his unchangeable God.

How can someone who is depressed rejoice? In 2 Timothy 1 Paul tells Timothy that he is mindful of Timothy's faith and of the faith of those before him. He reminds Timothy of who he is. "For this reason [based on who you are] I remind you to fan into flame the gift of God. . . . For God did not give us a spirit of timidity, but a spirit of power, of love and of self-discipline" (vv. 6—7). The spirit here refers to the dominant tendency of the mind. We are not talking about a feeling, but an attitude of the mind. It is an attitude that says you are a person created by God, a joint-heir with Christ, and an important part of his body. It is an attitude that leads to actions: "I will break through this mood."

Only as we set our minds on who we are and on exercising that "spirit of power, of love and of self-discipline," will our emotions be excluded from being the ruling force in our lives. This does not mean that negative feelings will be absent from our lives but rather that in spite of them Christ will become the ruling force that enables us to walk in a way that honors him.

It is my prayer that you and your husband together will hold tightly to this truth in the midst of your very difficult circumstances and that, as God leads you in the direction he would have your lives go, he will use these times to make you more like himself.

Dear Diane,

My husband is a seminary student interning at a local church. We hear many comments from other seminary couples and from those already in the ministry about problems we can expect to face when my husband becomes a pastor. Frankly, it is a bit overwhelming. We do not want to enter the pastorate naïvely, but neither do we want to be as negative as some appear to be. What problems should we expect to face? Will it be more difficult to maintain a good marriage while pastoring than if my husband had chosen a different career? Perhaps you could give us a realistic overview. Any suggestions (or warnings) will be appreciated.

Sincerely,
Beth

CHAPTER 11

How Should I Respond to a Husband Who Does Not Practice What He Preaches?

It is painful to watch someone we love choose a path that is destructive. Fear is added to that pain when the outcome could adversely affect our own future. Your anxiety about your husband is not at all irrational. His behavior warrants your concern. I hope to give you a better understanding of what your husband is doing and some suggestions to help you respond more constructively.

I will not deal with the pros and cons of drinking. Instead I will limit myself to discussing the problems your husband is exhibiting and to considering the most appropriate response.

Obviously, you are concerned about your husband's drinking, and indeed, you should be. To say a man has an occasional drink in his home is one thing; to say he is drinking in bars until the wee hours of the morning is quite another. At the very least, your husband is a potential alcoholic. He is consistently using alcohol as an escape and does not appear to view his behavior as a problem. One constructive way for you to deal with this is to join Al-Anon, the family branch of Alcoholics Anonymous. I would hope that you could attend a group where you would not be recognized as "the pastor's wife," for I assume such recognition would be difficult for you.

One of the things Al-Anon will teach you is that when a spouse is engaged in destructive behavior, a loved one will tend to cover for him or her, to step in and prevent the negative consequences that would ordinarily occur. An example of this would be the wife who calls the office repeatedly to say her husband is sick, when, in fact, he has a hangover.

This response may seem to help, but it will only exacerbate the problem. Someone who abuses alcohol has difficulty accepting responsibility. If that person's irresponsible behavior is covered up, there are no consequences to be faced, and that makes it easier for him or her to continue the destructive pattern.

I realize the challenge it is for a loved one to refuse to cover up. In your case it may mean disgrace for your husband and yourself and loss of a job. That possibility produces great anxiety and makes it very difficult to pull back. However, if you try to help your husband avoid consequences, you will only increase the problem.

Another important point that seems to stand out in your situation is that alcoholism is symptomatic. Your husband's drinking behavior is indicative of other problems. I am struck both by the fact that your husband is a pastor in a denomination that does not condone drinking and that he continues to drink in the face of your obvious distress. In effect, he is choosing a behavior that shows no concern for the desires of those important to him. It is safe to assume that his father would not approve; his denomination to whom he must answer does not approve; and, clearly, neither do you. Needless to say, God also does not approve of a blatant disregard for the desires and beliefs of others. Your husband seems to have trouble dealing with authority and with the approval or disapproval of those who are important to him.

It is crucial for you to recognize two additional facts. One is that you are not responsible for your husband's behavior. You may feel at times as if you are at fault, but the responsibility lies at his feet. The second is that you cannot change your husband. No amount of pleading, nagging, criticizing, or rational discussion will make your husband different. If you try to make him change, his resistance to you will only increase, and so will the behavior you are fighting.

Our ministry to our spouse or to any other believer is not to bring about conviction and change. Scripture tells us those jobs belong to the Holy Spirit. We see in John 16 that the Helper sent to us will convict concerning sin, righteousness, and judgment. God will often use us in this ministry of conviction, but it is not our job to convict. Paul states our job in 2 Corinthians 5:18: God has given us the "ministry of reconciliation." As we walk in obedience to God's Word, having our speech and actions controlled by his love, the Holy Spirit is free to convict another and to use us to bring about that person's reconciliation to God. So often our nagging and criticism make it difficult for another to be reconciled to God. First, because we, by our noise, drown out the Holy Spirit. Second, because the person being criticized and pushed will use his energies in defense against us and will not be free to respond to that still, small voice.

A woman I know was married to a man who was doing many wrong things. I agreed that they were wrong and that judgment was clearly supported by Scripture. Unfortunately, her reaction to his behavior was to daily inform him of his errors and tell him what a horrible sinner he was. The response to this was a week-by-week increment in those behaviors.

You see, the focus shifts from "How can I get my *husband* to change?" to "What is a godly response for *me* in these circumstances?" For instance, "What kind of response is appropriate when my husband drinks too much? What is a godly response when my husband preaches on Ephesians 5 and comes home and treats me terribly? What kind of response would God have me give when the man I am married to lives in contradiction to what he teaches?"

Oswald Chambers, in his devotional *My Utmost for His Highest,* gives some insight into what our attitude should be: "God gives us discernment, not so that we may criticize, but rather so that we may intercede." Whenever God gives us discernment in the life of a husband, child, or another Christian, he has done so for a purpose. That purpose is so that we may intercede on behalf of that person. We misuse God's gift of discernment by our pushing and pulling as we try to make others obey God.

Now, I am not saying that loving confrontation is inappropriate. However, loving confrontation does not consist of a daily occurrence of nagging, pleading, and put-downs. Yes, we need to say:

> I am troubled by the contradiction between what God's Word says and what I see in your life. I know you want God to bless your ministry and that you want to honor him by your obedience to his Word. I believe your (such-and-such) behavior is not in accordance with what Scripture says. Could we pray together about this? Perhaps I am wrong and God can show me that. I only desire that both of us might grow together in him.

That is not a critical statement, nor is it filled with anger and resentment. We are free to respond in this manner only when we have prayed *much,* both for our spouse and for our own heart attitude. For if we are bitter and angry, we sin as much against God as our partner has.

The next step, after much prayer and a loving statement of what we perceive as a problem, is that we must go back to prayer and a tongue that is slow to speak. We must let God strive with the one we have talked to, all the while keeping our hearts free of resentment. Then the Holy Spirit is free to do his work, and we are effective ministers of reconciliation.

I will pray for you and your husband that in this frustrating and difficult conflict God will continually bring you both into conformity to his Word.

Dear Diane,

My husband and I have been married for almost ten years. We both desire a healthy and happy sexual relationship, but instead we are experiencing great frustration in this area. Our frustration has reached a point where we have reconciled ourselves to having sex only once or twice a month. The reason for our dissatisfaction is my lack of a physical response. When we were first married, I had little difficulty reaching an orgasm, but as the pressures of seminary increased, satisfaction came to me less and less. It has now been years since I have found any physical release in our lovemaking. I enjoy being with my husband and loving him, but our frustration has begun to override even the pleasures of that aspect. Can you give us some guidelines to help us recapture what we had in the beginning of our marriage?

Sincerely,
Carol

CHAPTER 12

How Can We Find a Healthy Sexual Relationship?

I am pleased by your forthrightness and your courage to ask for help in an area where so many Christians are silent. Certainly the door to discussion is more open now than ever before, but many still have great difficulty saying, "That's my problem." Your willingness to do so is a big step toward dealing with your situation. Your letter may also encourage others with sexual struggles and enable them to speak more openly in their own marriages.

Christians should not be afraid to deal with the subject of sex. We know that God has given us the gift of sex and that what he gives is good. How this gift translates into the specifics of our individual marriages, however, is often lost in the shuffle. The sexual aspect of marriage should provide an oasis amid the tumult and mundaneness of everyday living. A man and a woman need such a place apart to relax and enjoy each other without pressure, fear, or embarrassment. Your letter indicates that both you and your husband view sex from a healthy perspective. Needless to say, this is a requisite for you to have a fulfilling sexual relationship. When a husband or wife views sex as a duty to be endured or a source of guilt, fear, or embarrassment, problems and dissatisfaction occur. Let us provide more in the way of context before we look at practical suggestions that you and your husband could pursue.

In Genesis 2:23 Adam called Eve "bone of my bones and flesh of my flesh." Paul elaborates on this in Ephesians 5 when he says that a man and his wife are one flesh. He goes even further in defining this in 1 Corinthians 7:4, "The wife's body does not belong to her alone but also to her husband. In the same way, the husband's body does not belong to him alone but also to his wife."

This means many things both spiritually and practically. I would like to concentrate on a couple of these. First, Scripture provides us with a focus that is clearly opposed to the philosophy of today. The world says to seek your own pleasure or do what feels good. God says to bring all your energies to bear on seeking your partner's pleasure. Cherish your partner; keep his or her interests as your priority. Certainly this means that we are to please our spouses in things that are sexual, but it also includes such aspects as timing, atmosphere, attitudes in the home, speed, and everything else that affects this oasis.

Second, it removes the focus on the end result— not that the result of orgasm is unimportant but rather that it is not central. What becomes central in the context of what God says is the *process* of loving each other. It is a process that involves the entirety of the day and simply spills over into the bedroom. This process of loving is to be characterized by gentleness, thoughtfulness, and kindness. You must not accept infrequent or frustrating sex as your lot. In doing so, you will have lost sight of your loving as a process rather than as a means to an end. You will also have allowed your frustration with one aspect to override the benefits of all your loving together.

Unfortunately, you have become entrenched in a vicious circle. Due to your circumstances, approaching sex likely evokes a certain level of tension in both of you. In order to circumvent this cycle, you must go back to the beginning. Let the idea of orgasm go; assume it to be something you need not concern yourselves with, as prior to marriage. In other words, do not seek it; it is something for a later time.

Start with an extended time without sex so that you can relearn the beginnings of loving without pressure. You mentioned that you think seminary and its accompanying difficulties may have interfered with establishing a good sexual relationship, so go back to premarital loving. Spend a week touching each other in passing, holding hands, and hugging and kissing each other a lot. Do nothing more than this so that there is no expectation and no pressure to continue. Use great care and gentleness with each other and try never to be in a hurry. Have a lot of lovely, long hugs and kisses, and enjoy them for what they are rather than as a prelude to sex.

After you have done this and find it fun, relaxing, and stimulating, move on to the next stage. This stage consists of continuing the above and extending it to include leisurely time together without clothes, gently exploring each other's bodies, excluding the genital area and not proceeding to intercourse. Do this for several days or more until it is also enjoyable and relaxing to both of you.

Go on from the above to the next step, continuing

what you have been doing but now including the genital areas. Again, do not proceed to intercourse, but enjoy this time and find relaxation in it.

Finally, allow all that you have enjoyed together in a relaxing way to move naturally into intercourse. The key is to provide a relaxed atmosphere and to proceed at a pace dictated by your level of comfort. There is no hurry because you have the rest of your lives together. I would think your ability to relax and enjoy all this would be greatly enhanced by whittling away as many extra commitments and social engagements as possible. Take a month out of your lives and slow way down. Go out to romantic dinners together; take long walks; listen to music; enjoy quiet evenings at home with no television and no phone. You are investing in a lifetime relationship for one month, and the returns should be great.

Focus on loving each other, surprising each other with thoughtfulness, encouraging each other, and exploring each other's bodies. As you do this step by step with no expectations of achieving a certain performance level, you should find yourselves happily learning to love each other in a creative and unique way. Look at your relationship as a dance together. It will be unlike any other couple's, for you are unique individuals. Bring all your creative energies to bear on your lives together, and see what you can do to increase your delight at belonging to one another.

As you follow through with the steps outlined above, you will find great joy in the process of loving and pleasuring each other. Let your focus continually be on your spouse, always asking, "How can I bring pleasure to him/her with my attitudes, my talk, and my body?" As you do this together, the physical release will follow sometime down the road. Do not let orgasm be your focus. Enjoy it when it is there, but do not seek it. Instead, seek to enjoy each other to the fullest as you spend the rest of your lives fine-tuning the instrument of your marriage.

Sometimes a problem becomes so entrenched that it requires professional intervention. Many large hospitals have sex clinics that help with problems such as yours. If careful adherence to the steps outlined above does not bring satisfactory results, I would strongly encourage you and your husband to seek some professional help. Often, clinics are set up so that couples from out of town can come and stay for several days while receiving counseling. This way you need not feel embarrassed because of knowing those from whom you are seeking help.

May God bless you as you grow in this process we call marriage.

Dear Diane,

My husband is a minister. I am in the process of desperately trying to recover from an affair with a man who works closely with my husband. This man has been a leader in our church and has personal qualities that I admire and respect. We had a long-term and very close relationship, though nothing physical occurred during that time. The relationship ended because both he and I knew that it was wrong and potentially very dangerous to our marriages and to the church. However, I still see this man in church regularly and, due to other circumstances in his home, I have been actively ministering to his wife and children. My husband was aware of the relationship and of my love for this man. He was hurt by it, but we had a realistic discussion about our marriage, and now he seems content. I ended the relationship because I value the reputation of my husband within the church community, and I did not want to do anything to harm him. The pain and loneliness and depression that I am experiencing, though the relationship ended almost two years ago, are very devastating to me. Am I doing something wrong that it is taking me so long to get over this man and get on with my life? I was seeing a counselor, whom I found very beneficial, but unfortunately he has moved away. Any advice you can offer will be greatly appreciated.

Thank you.

Very sincerely,
Sandy

CHAPTER 13

How Can I Recover
From an Affair?

P salm 25:16−17 seems to express similar feelings to those in your letter: "Turn to me and be gracious to me, for I am lonely and afflicted. The troubles of my heart have multiplied; free me from my anguish."

It strikes me, in reading your letter, that the central issue is not so much your present dilemma but rather your continued pain. I sense discouragement, loneliness, and depression in your letter, as well as your feeling that these emotions will go on and on. The pain is a theme you return to again and again, and that is what we must focus on.

When pain (physical or emotional) continues after we have pursued reasonable means to alleviate it, it is time to ask ourselves some questions. An obvious one, which I am sure you have already asked is: "Are there other things I could do to help eliminate my distress?" Another way of posing this question is: "Can I find anything I might be doing that could be increasing my sadness?" Let's look at this possibility before going on to further questions.

You have certainly not waited passively for things to change, and that is good. You have looked at some difficult circumstances and have taken steps to control them. You backed off from this man and spent some time seeing a counselor. You were wise to take both of these steps. I do wonder about your continuing relationship with this man's wife and children, however. You have made a decision not to be involved with him but continue to feel ambivalent about that decision. Any involvement with his family at this time, especially in a supportive role, will serve only to increase your ambivalence and make it more difficult to let go. Avoiding any personal contact with this man and his family may help make your decision to be more clearcut and firm. If this family needs the support and contact you have provided, lovingly direct them to someone else.

Another important question for us to consider is: "Is the real source of my pain what I have assumed it to be, or could it lie elsewhere?" Because of your attraction to this man—your respect for him and your sadness at walking away from him—you have understandably felt that he (or your feelings for him) is the source of your difficulty. However, the continued intensity of your pain suggests that, instead of looking externally, you might profit by looking inward.

Often we carry around a sense of unhappiness about which we remain unaware until external events bring it to the forefront. There are a couple of things in your letter that suggest this is a good possibility in your case. One of these is the comments you made about your relationship to your husband. You mentioned that you value the reputation of your husband's job. You also said that your husband seems content, that he assumes everything is okay, and that you and your husband had a "realistic" discussion about your own marriage. These statements both puzzle and concern me. I do not have any feel from your letter for the kind of marriage you have, but the references you did make to your husband (as well as your omissions) suggest some sadness and perhaps resignation to a relationship that is less than what you hoped for.

I wonder whether you were attracted to this man because his leadership and personal qualities embodied the dynamic leader you had hoped to marry. There is a feeling of distance as well as of passivity in your statements about your husband's assumption that things are all right. Surely your pain of the past two years has been evident in the way you live, talk, and show love to your husband. How do you feel about his conclusions regarding something that has been so important and difficult for you? Did you perhaps feel he was too quick or too willing to forgive and forget? It must have been painful for him to learn of your regard for this other man with whom he works on a continual basis. Your husband's apparent contentment may simply be a mask that prevents him from facing what he fears.

Your own fears are another area for consideration. Frequently, a spouse who is dissatisfied in a marriage tends to deny that unhappiness for fear of the potential consequences. Such dissatisfactions tend to smolder, however, and when they finally do surface, they often take the form of depression or an affair. In either case, these external manifestations are not really the problem but are only symptoms of an unrecognized dismay about one's own marriage.

Though you speak about your husband, you say nothing of the quality of your marriage nor of your feelings toward him and communication with him.

Your mention of a "realistic" discussion suggests a feeling of resignation to a relationship that is less than you want. You say that you "value your husband's reputation" but not that you value him. You have actively fought against a relationship with this other man, but it seems that you have not actively pursued building up your marriage. I believe this is the key to why your pain has been so prolonged. You will begin to find relief not only as you continue turning *from* a potential affair, but also if you continually turn *to* your marriage. Your feeling that you are trapped will recede only when you are free to actively pursue a fulfilling relationship with your husband. Otherwise, you are indeed trapped. You risk continuing your marriage to a man not for love of him but for fear of leaving him. Meanwhile, the man you want will grow larger than life as you fantasize a relationship with him. Your husband will be fighting a losing battle, for he can never compete with the fantasy man to whom you have given yourself.

Handling all of this will mean more pain and will be far from easy. It is not something I would recommend you to attempt on your own. I am very sorry your counselor has moved away, and I strongly suggest that you begin seeing another one. First you must go alone and deal with the reality of your life and the choices you have made. Once you have come first to an acceptance and then to a commitment to the choices and the people they include, you and your husband must see a good marriage counselor. There is much to be done in the areas of communication, common goals regarding your relationship together, and a willing commitment to loving and accepting each other. God has given you to each other, and he would have you to "make every effort to keep the unity of the Spirit" (Eph. 4:3) in your marriage. Not only do you have a promise to each other to uphold before God, but also you should be a model of a godly marriage before your congregation.

A woman I counseled for a long time was in circumstances very similar to yours. She found it difficult to face her rejection of her marriage and the kind of man she had chosen. However, with time and a strong commitment to honoring that choice for the glory of God, she came to accept and, finally, to enjoy her husband.

Again, much lies before you that is difficult, but you can claim the promise of Psalm 34:18: "The LORD is close to the brokenhearted and saves those who are crushed in spirit." You must not forget this as you turn and set your mind on what must be done. Verse 4 of the same psalm says, "I sought the LORD, and he answered me; he delivered me from all my fears." You are not alone, and you are not trapped, for you have a sympathetic High Priest who is also your Deliverer. In his strength you can face the future with courage, and by his might you can walk fully, and not in resignation, in the way that he has for you.

Dear Diane,

   At a recent meeting for pastors in our denomination many of the wives came together to share ideas and problems. One of the difficulties mentioned by several of the women had to do with their location. These women (I am one of them) live in small, rural towns. Everyone knows everyone else. At times we have felt unable to handle a problem on our own. We did not want to use the only Christian counselor in town because he went to our church. What suggestions can you offer us that might be helpful in such circumstances?

Sincerely,
Alissa

CHAPTER 14
Where Can I Go for Help?

Finding good support and counsel is not always easy in the best of circumstances. When you are the pastor's wife, you live "out in the sticks," and the only Christian counselor within a hundred-mile radius attends your church, the problem seems insurmountable. This difficulty is common to many ministry wives and is often mentioned in discussions at pastoral seminars.

I am afraid there is no easy answer. Even a list of guidelines for finding good counsel will not cover all circumstances. Regardless of what I might suggest, some women will still have to struggle through a problem alone. In an effort to keep that number at a minimum, I will offer some suggestions that have been used by many women in circumstances similar to yours.

There are two important points that need to be made at the outset. Psychological depression is what often overwhelms people and causes them to seek professional help. When biological signs (poor appetite, sleep disturbance, loss of energy, and others) accompany depression, or when emotional symptoms are severe, the disorder will often respond to medication. Any counselor that you consult should be able to recognize the indications for treating depression and other psychological disorders with medication as well as with counseling. The counselor that you select should know when it is appropriate to refer you for medical evaluation and medication. Too often Christians assume that there is solely a spiritual cause for depression. Certainly depression can be due to wrong behavior or sinfulness that results in a spiritually depressed state. But depression and other psychological disorders can be related to physical problems as well, and this aspect also needs to be considered.

We are "fearfully and wonderfully made," and we have much yet to learn regarding the interdependency of the physical, emotional, mental, and spiritual components of life. We need to be careful and to exercise great wisdom in this area. We will make mistakes, harmful to ourselves and others, if we make general assumptions about our problems. Certainly we do not want to pursue a course without considering God's perspective on the matter. Neither do we want to mindlessly give an answer that is to be considered applicable to all situations for all time. Let me give two examples.

A woman who had been depressed for some time came to see me several years ago. She struggled with very low self-esteem and wanted me to "help her feel better." It turned out that she was and continued to be blatantly involved in an adulterous relationship, but she refused to see any connection between that action and her bad feelings. Obviously, sometimes despair is

God-given. God uses our lack of well-being to say, "There is a problem, or sin, in your life. Let's deal with it." Such feelings can have the same effect as physical pain. When your hand starts to hurt, you remove it from the hot pan. The pain causes you to notice the error you are committing. Mental and emotional pain can have the same function. However, as with physical pain, such agony can occur for reasons over which you have no control.

Another woman came to my office extremely depressed. She had terrible guilt over her depression and had been severely chastised for being depressed. Because of the nature and severity of her symptoms, I insisted that she see a physician for a complete physical examination. She was found to be in the early stages of a medical disease that was contributing to her depression. When this woman was given the proper medication, her depression was alleviated.

I say all this to stress that we must carefully and lovingly assess ourselves and/or others before we make a judgment regarding the cause of the pain and the best cure for it.

My second point relates to your statement that the only Christian counselor in town attends your church. Often there is a fear among both ministers and their wives about revealing problems to church members. Just because a counselor attends your church does not mean that you should not see that person or that that person cannot help you. There are times when the nature of the problem precludes seeking such help, or you may believe that seeking counsel might weaken or cause other difficulties for the counselor. However, beyond that there is no reason not to see those whom you serve. They are gifted by God to serve you as well, and God has structured the body so that there can be mutual servanthood. The minister and his wife are not excluded from this mutuality. Pride should never be the reason that you hesitate to seek help from someone you know and must face on Sunday.

Having presented these two thoughts for your consideration, let me go on to list some ideas that other ministry wives have found helpful.

One solution some have used successfully when no counselor is in close proximity is to find one that is some distance away and go with less frequency. One woman I know went to see a counselor once a month during a difficult stage in her life. The counselor was three hours away. She and her husband arranged their budgets and schedules so that she could go and see the counselor, spend the night away, and then see her again in the morning and return home before the children were out of school.

Other women have received help from other pastors in their town. They have counseled with the minister of another congregation, knowing that their confidences would be kept and benefiting from the minister's knowledge of the difficulties of pastoral life.

Many ministry wives sing the praises of other ministry wives as excellent sources of support and wise counsel. It has been my experience that few denominations encourage this among the pastors' wives within their group. I know of none who do so across denominational lines. I have urged many women to seek support from each other. It has given me great pleasure through the years to hear of relationships between pastors' wives that have enabled many to better weather hard times. I know a woman from a tiny town in the Midwest who made a point of establishing a friendship with the wife of another pastor in town. They pursued outside interests together and nurtured their friendship along. Several years later this woman found herself in a crisis situation, and it was that friendship that carried her through. Another pastor's wife in a rural Canadian town met and liked a woman she met at a pastors' conference. They corresponded for years and used tapes instead of letters when the need to talk was strong. These are not ideal solutions, perhaps, but they have proved valuable to many.

Finally, I suggest that you seek the wisdom of the written word. While this does not fill the need for a helping relationship, reading books regarding your area of struggle can offer a sorely needed perspective other than your own. Many ministry wives find help and support in *Partnership,* a magazine specifically geared to their needs (465 Gundersen Drive, Carol Stream, IL 60188).

When all is said and done, there will be many ministry wives in need of counsel and encouragement who will find themselves in circumstances that do not seem to provide for such needs. It is my earnest prayer that during such times the reality of God's presence and unconditional love will be wonderfully evident. Scripture is full of such promises, and in the darkest hour we must fight to hold to the truth of such verses. Whatever our circumstances, God has called us to glorify him and to serve others. As we continue on in this way, the psalmist says that when "the righteous cry out, and the LORD hears them; he delivers them from all their troubles. The LORD is close to the broken-hearted and saves those who are crushed in spirit" (34:17—18).

DATE DUE